The Lean Book
of Lean

The Lean Book of Lean

A Concise Guide to Lean
Management for Life
and Business

John A. A. Earley

WILEY

Registered office
John Wiley & Sons Ltd, The Atrium, Southern Gate, Chichester, West Sussex, PO19 8SQ, United Kingdom

For details of our global editorial offices, for customer services and for information about how to apply for permission to reuse the copyright material in this book please visit our website at www.wiley.com.

Library of Congress Cataloging-in-Publication Data is available

A catalogue record for this book is available from the British Library.

ISBN 978-1-119-09619-1 (pbk) ISBN 978-1-119-09620-7 (ebk)
ISBN 978-1-119-09621-4 (ebk) ISBN 978-1-119-27170-3 (ebk)

Cover Design: Kathy Davis/Wiley
Cover Image: © singpentinkhappy/Shutterstock

Set in 10/13.5pt SabonLTStd by Aptara Inc., New Delhi, India
Printed in Great Britain by TJ International Ltd, Padstow, Cornwall, UK

CONTENTS

Contents

ACKNOWLEDGEMENTS

Without the help, support and inspiration from those around me throughout my life, this book would never have been written and my life would have been very different. While there are many who have guided, prodded and cajoled me into what I am, there are a few people to whom I would like to specifically say a big "thank you" in the context of this book.

Firstly, my wife Helen, who has supported and put up with me for over 30 years and kept believing in me, even when things haven't gone quite according to plan.

To Jim Prendergast, a Partner with PricewaterhouseCoopers, who recognised the Lean in me and let me loose to practise and develop my skills. His mentorship helped me to turn some good concepts and rough thoughts into practical approaches to helping people see the light. To the others in the "Lean Team" at PwC who were instrumental in a lot of the thinking behind this book.

To James C. Paterson, author of *Lean Auditing* and a colleague from my time at AstraZeneca. James very kindly introduced me to his contact at Wiley which opened the door to turning a pipe dream into reality. To Gemma from Wiley who sponsored this book and has been very patient with me during the writing and publishing process.

Thank you all for your help, support and encouragement.

PREFACE

W hy did I choose to call this book *The Lean Book of Lean*? Having attempted to read many of the books published on the subject, I always found myself unable to finish them. That's not to say that they are irrelevant, badly written or uninteresting, it is just that with the little time available to your average busy person, there is always something which takes priority. I often questioned, why doesn't someone write a book which covers the major points, has some useful hints and tips, but can be read during your average 3 to 4 hour flight? (And have time for your in-flight drink as well!) After many years pondering this issue, I came to the conclusion that the "someone" might as well be me.

As more of an afterthought, but just as relevant, Lean is all about achieving a desired outcome with the minimal amount of fuss and effort, so I felt compelled to write a book which practises what it preaches.

In addition, I have become increasingly frustrated over the years with learned people and scholars trying to make out that Lean is magic, something only they can easily understand. I'm on slightly shaky ground here as I'm a consultant myself and have made a more than decent living from helping others "get it" so could be considered as one of the culprits mentioned above. To try and break this myth, I've tried to explain the concepts and principles in everyday terms and demonstrate that we all "do Lean" naturally in our everyday lives. In a light-hearted vein, I've also added a glossary in the back defining some of the key Lean terms in the same way.

Just to be very clear from the outset, I have not done extended research or interviewed all the "gods of Lean" to create this book. It is a collection of my own thoughts, experiences and, in some cases, opinions of the subject. I don't pretend to know everything. I don't profess to be right about anything. What I do have is 30 years of experience and battle scars of helping others on their journey, which I'm offering up for the price of this book.

So here it is: *The Lean Book of Lean*. Able to be read on your average flight (well, if you're a fast reader or take long flights!). Not the definitive compendium of Lean and all its facets, but hopefully sufficient to leave you motivated and confident that anyone can do it, and yes, that means you! Take what you want, discard what you don't need or don't agree with, but I hope you find it useful in some way and that it gives you a little food for thought in whatever capacity you live your life and for whatever reason you picked up this book.

Thanks for your time and interest.

INTRODUCTION TO LEAN

Welcome to *The Lean Book of Lean*: a not-too-daunting volume about a subject that has been the subject of ebbs and flows of popularity over the last three decades. Lean has seemed to reinvent itself over and over with a few name changes along the way. To some, it's a silver bullet capable of saving the world as we know it; to others it's had its day and should move over and let the new silver bullet take the limelight. To others still, it's just a name for a collection of tools that have been around a long time and seem to be of some practical use. For me? Well, I'm inclined towards the last group. Enough of this philosophical wittering, I've only got 70,000 words to play with, so on with the book!

In this first chapter we will do a brief exploration into what Lean is, where it can be applied and what certified level of Master Wizard you need to achieve to be confident you can apply it without destroying the universe.

The definition of Lean

"Lean Production is 'lean' because it uses less of everything when compared to mass production – half the manufacturing space, half the investment in tools, half the engineering hours to develop a new product in half the time. Also, it requires keeping far less than half the needed inventory on site, results in many fewer defects, and produces a greater and ever growing variety of productions."

MIT's International Motor Vehicles Program (IMVP)

"'Lean' is not a new concept. If you are reducing inventory, expanding jobs and responsibilities, participating on a multi-functional work team, benchmarking, or creating and maintaining relationships with customers, then you are practicing a part of lean production."

The Lean Aerospace Initiative (LAI)

"Lean Manufacturing is a manufacturing philosophy which shortens the time between the customer order and the product build/shipment by eliminating sources of waste."

Mr John Shook

"TPS (what is now called Lean in some quarters) is a manufacturing phenomenon that seeks to maximize the work effort of a company's number one resource, the People. Lean is therefore a way of thinking to adapt to change, eliminate waste, and continuously improve."

Mr Ohno in a discussion with Mr Cho: Toyota Motor Manufacturing Company

"Thin: lacking excess flesh"

www.wordnetweb.princeton.edu

The above are just a few definitions of Lean that I picked up from a quick trawl of the Internet; there are literally hundreds out there, each concocted to send a specific message to the audiences in mind. I particularly like the last one as it is closest to the true meaning of the word and less wrapped up in jargon, in other words, Lean. To me, the best definition of what we are talking about here – one I've used a lot and will refer back to a few times throughout this book – is summed up by the lazy person's approach to life:

"Doing the absolute minimum necessary to get the desired result."

Lazy or smart? In my opinion, the successful lazy person has to be smart to figure out how to get away with it, so probably both. The way I see it, as long as you keep this principle in mind at all times when you are looking for improvement opportunities, you won't go far wrong. However, does this mean cutting corners, shoddy work and dissatisfaction with your performance in the eyes of those around you and your "customers"? No, not if you define "desired result" correctly. This is the one most critical part of any Lean application: defining the outcome you are looking for. Although this seems obvious, it never ceases to amaze me how many businesses embark on an improvement programme without a clear understanding of what they are trying to achieve. We will cover this in the next chapter in some depth, so enough on this for now.

Lean – the natural order of living

Many consultants, "black belts" and business leaders would like us to believe that Lean is some mystical state of mind, something which takes years of experience and astute business know-how to understand or implement. But I don't believe this is true, the evidence is all around us that Lean is a natural way of working for us, not something we have to study and practise devoutly for decades to understand. This one issue, the common belief that Lean is somehow magic, is the biggest blocker to progress in my opinion, the main reason it takes so long sometimes for the light bulb to come on. I've heard time and time again, "It can't be that simple" but yes it is, really it is.

To prove the point, let's take an everyday example, and on the way introduce some Lean jargon.

The shopping trip

All of us have done it – been to the supermarket for the food shopping. OK, so what, you might say, not much to think about there is there, and what has food shopping got to do with running a Lean business? But let's take a step back and think about the process a bit more.

What's the objective? To use scarce resources, your money and your time, to get all you need to run a house and feed a family for a few days.

Any parallels so far? Well, consider the resources: money and people; businesses use those, and both are always in short supply. Stuff to run a house and feed the family can be considered as buying supplies and raw materials, to be made into products for your family, sorry, customers. OK, it seems to work so far.

Now for the process. Most people going food shopping do some checking first to see what's needed before setting off, then create a list, either literally or subconsciously. The trick is getting the right amount. Too little and the kids start complaining about the lack of dinner, too much and the stuff won't fit in the fridge or goes off before you can use it. How do you do this? You look in the cupboards and the fridge and, based on what's there and your knowledge of how much you generally use in the periods between shopping trips, figure out what needs to be bought to last you through to the next time you go shopping. Oh, by the way, you just remembered that Granny is coming to stay for the weekend so you will need some extra milk, eggs and a larger piece of meat.

This is all so obvious and natural that most people can do it, and for the seasoned food shopper, it happens even without thinking about it. But we have introduced some very important Lean concepts here, so let's go over it again from a business point of view: Understanding the right level of inventory to support demand but avoid write-off, slow-moving and obsolete stock, based on historical demand. That's all about the core Lean concept of the Inventory Control Point (ICP) or Strategic Buffer Replenishment model of supply, where you periodically look at your current inventory and replenish back to the top of the buffer. The buffer is calculated based on historical demand and trends: a forecast. Just like when we go shopping, we might know that, on average, we use four litres of milk between shopping trips (the forecast) but that doesn't mean that we blindly go out and buy four litres every time we go shopping: we take a look in the fridge and realise that we ought to top up to five litres (four on average, plus one so we don't run out if we overuse); see there are two left and only buy three. The forecast is a guide, not something we execute blindly. Oh, and the Granny visit? That's adjusting the buffer for known events as part of the Event Management Process. No known events, just maintain the status quo, no need for a complicated planning session.

Now let's take a closer look at what the fridge does. The fridge is the buffer between the supply of food and the family, allowing periodic shopping trips and absorbing variability in the consumption of food. It's also a visible trigger that a shopping trip is necessary as the supply of critical foods gets low. In Lean terms, the fridge is a very effective kanban.

These simple mechanisms allow shopping trips to be made at regular intervals, the right amounts of food to be bought on each trip and avoid wasting food. The key thing here, though, is that this works perfectly without having to know in advance exactly what everyone is going to eat over the next week. In other words, the forecast does not have to be accurate at a detailed level, only at a macro demand level. The kanban (fridge), real time shopping list and relatively frequent shopping trips handle the day-to-day variability automatically.

However, just one cautionary footnote before we delve into more detail. As I'm sure everyone has experienced, sometimes this can all go wrong. The fridge is full with food all close to the use-by date and the things you want are just not there, or buried under this pile of soon-to-be-trashed food. Why did this happen, if it's such an effective Lean tool? Does this mean that everything said so far is just mumbo-jumbo and doesn't work in the real world? Well, let's take a look at what probably happened here.

When you take a closer look at what that expired stuff is before you chuck it all in the bin and reflect on all the wasted cash, we see a couple of recurring themes.

Firstly, a lot of it is the dreaded "impulse buy", in other words, a lot of stuff you never really needed in the first place. Secondly, you'll find several packs of the same thing and if you cast your mind back you'll probably remember the "three for the price of two" deal on at the time, persuading you to part with your money to get something free. In reality it's not as free as you first thought, as you end up paying for two when you really needed one and end up throwing at least one away. All of these problems are as a result of caving in to the devious antics of the supermarket marketing ploys, which waste your money and fridge space but keep them in business.

Yes, but this is just silly shoppers being duped, right? Real business people don't fall for this do they? Really? Never heard of instances where Purchasing get a good deal by buying larger quantities of something that sits on the shelf for the next three years?

The bottom line here is discipline. This is at the heart of Lean thinking and good shopping or business management. If you don't stick to the rules, all the best ideas and processes in the world won't save you.

So there you have it. We all do some Lean in our everyday lives and we don't even think about it. Basic common sense, I hear you say, and indeed it is. This is just one example of Lean concepts showing up in everyday life – there are many more if you stop and think about it. So why do businesses have so much trouble and employ armies of people to do something that simple? In my experience, small entrepreneurial companies don't have this problem; they run their businesses like families and employ Lean concepts naturally, just like you and me. It's the bigger guys who seem to have the problem. Their sheer size, organisational structure and hierarchy seem to prevent them from behaving in a natural way. So we need to find a way to break through this constraint and get the organisation thinking like they do when they go home.

The first step in this is to define a small set of common sense-based principles that everyone can get their heads round and embrace.

2

THE CORE LEAN PRINCIPLES

As I've hinted at before, Lean is simple and there should only be a few principles that need to be kept in mind to be successful. In this chapter I will introduce a few that I believe are core to the thinking. None of this will be earth-shattering insights from the heavens for you, but it should at least make you think a bit about how the parts fit together. So, here they are:

- Be customer demand-driven – Don't do anything until there is demand from the customer to do it.
- Maximise flow – Once something has been started, finish it. After all, if you apply the rule above, someone wants it now, so why hold it up?
- Identify and eliminate waste – Learn to identify waste in all its forms: material, time and resources. Then take whatever steps necessary to eliminate it.
- Declare war on variation – Variability kills. It creates an atmosphere of uncertainty, which causes much of the waste mentioned above. Systematically identify and eliminate the root cause, not just the symptoms.
- Organise your people around outcomes you want – Create an organisational structure around delivery of your products or services to customers. Make sure there is clear individual or team accountability for end-to-end delivery.

- Equip your people, at all levels, with the skills to be successful in their roles.

- Clear and simple measures and controls – Lean environments are fast and things happen very quickly, so you need to keep aware of the situation and have early warning indicators at critical points in the business.

- Finally, paint a clear and compelling picture of what the future looks and feels like in your "Ideal State" – then tell everyone!

This last point is absolutely critical. Without a clear understanding of where you are going, your organisation will flounder around and find its own destinations, which probably will not be consistent with the objectives of the business and certainly not consistent with each other. A favourite quote of mine by a certain grinning cat from a well-known children's book sums this up perfectly: "If you don't know where you're going, any road will get you there"[1]

If you start a change programme without a clear destination, when you get "there" it probably will not be where you really wanted to be and will have taken three times longer than you expected. Not good, so more on this later.

There are many other principles and rules that delve into detail on specific topics, but to me these are the cardinal ones, and are so fundamental that it is worth spending a little time to understand them in more detail. In keeping with the theme of this book, I'll try to provide examples in both the business context and in everyday life.

Be customer demand-driven

Sounds very obvious, but it's not always that easy. The first step is to understand who the customer is and what value means for that customer. Here are my definitions:

---

[1]From *Alice's Adventures in Wonderland* by Lewis Carroll.

The customer is an **external** person or organisation which ultimately **consumes/uses** your product or service. Not somebody who does something to it, then just passes it on.

This is the first hurdle you need to overcome and one at which many organisations fall. The history of Lean doesn't help here, in that many see it, and still refer to it, as Lean Manufacturing, implying that it's all about processes, and stops at the factory gates. Nothing could be further from the real truth and power of Lean. When starting out, don't constrain yourself to the internal view, always look at your business from the point of view of the external customer. In most businesses, the customer is the consumer of the products or services and, as most large businesses are publicly owned, the shareholders. In some industries, customers may include regulators and governments as well. Now we have "who the customer is" sorted, we need to take a look at value:

Value is something that the customer is prepared to **pay** or **sacrifice** for.

This might seem an odd phrase: "sacrifice for", but think about it. If you value something as an individual, you are prepared to make sacrifices to get it, keep it or care for it. The ultimate example is, of course, your family. What good parent wouldn't sacrifice everything for their child? The same is true in business: if you offer something of value to your customers, they'll very often do more than just part with money for it. They will use it, do without something else to get it, tell their friends about it and ultimately come back for more. All of which is good for your business.

Again, this all sounds very simple and obvious, but don't be complacent about it. In the complex world of big corporations, identifying the true customer and what they value can be a difficult task. It is vital, however, that you don't move on until you have this nailed, and please, please, please make sure that you validate your ideas with the customer to make sure.

So, we have customer value defined, which will help focus Lean on what is important. As a by-product, it will also help define new products and services to offer, but let's not go there right now as this is the Lean Book of Lean, not the Lean Encyclopedia!

With a clear handle on value, we should fire up the furnaces, get the engine in gear and start creating as much of it as possible, right? Well, not quite. Whatever "it" is, there is only value if there is current demand for it. If not, it's just going to sit around doing nothing at your expense until the demand miraculously appears, or it becomes obsolete and you have to give it, or throw it, away, wasting all that hard work which went into producing it in the first place.

A good example of this happened at a well-known fashion company, which embarked on a Lean Manufacturing programme that was an outstanding success: their productivity and production increased enormously and production costs plummeted. Unfortunately, they forgot about the demand-driven bit and linked their highly efficient production machine to the sales forecast created ahead of the season. Inevitably, actual sales did not match the forecast and they were left with frustrated customers who couldn't get the hot stuff they wanted, and warehouses full of the stuff that didn't really catch on. The result was that the lost orders and the cost of carrying and then writing off that excess inventory was ten times the savings they had made in the factory. When they looked back, they discovered that their shiny Lean factory actually wasn't agile enough to be capable of responding to the real demand as and when it materialised. They just did not think about Lean as something useful outside of the factory. We'll discuss the broader application of Lean compared to Lean Manufacturing a bit later.

So, the first principle of Lean is: **do nothing**, unless the customer requires you to do something, which usually comes in the form of an order. This is very hard sometimes, especially in an environment which is driven by traditional financial drivers, like overhead absorption, the killer of many a promising Lean programme. The pressure is on to keep the machines running, drive up utilisation and Overall Equipment Effectiveness (OEE). Lean is not necessarily in opposition to this, but puts a caveat on it: "if there is demand from the customer."

So, let's try to put a "real life" angle on this to see if it all stacks up. Ask yourself these simple questions, would you:

- Drive to pick up a friend from the other side of town on the off-chance they might want to come and visit you?
- Make a meal when no one is hungry?
- Go to fill up the tank when you're on full already, but it's Tuesday, fill-up day?

The answers here are obvious (hopefully!). The key thing here is to ask the question: Is there a real need for me to do this? Does someone need it?

Maximise flow

This is very simple in concept, but sometimes hard in practice. As mentioned above, this means that once you get the signal from the customer to start, stoke up the boilers, get the engines running and don't let anything get in the way until it's in the hands of the customer. At a local level this isn't too hard to do, but for a whole business, it isn't that easy. Look around the countryside at all the massive buildings dotted around with hundreds of truck-docking bays – those are warehouses. Each one filled to the gunwales with products waiting for somewhere to go or to be asked for by someone. In short: a testament to the failure of a business to maintain flow. To implement Lean properly, and get the full benefit for both you and your customers, the whole supply chain must be Lean, not just parts of it. If not, then you end up squeezing a balloon. One part gets thinner as you work on it and all that happens is that the waste you worked so hard to eliminate just pops out somewhere else and the net result is zero. I've seen so many times, Lean teams, site leaders and even COOs, clapping each other on the back saying how great their Lean programme is going and citing all the benefits delivered. However, the miserable old CFO is sitting in the corner looking at the company annual report, shaking his head and muttering to himself, "I don't see it here". And of course, the miserable old goat is right. All that's happened is that the waste has been redistributed and changed form, not been expelled from the business, largely because flow was not maximised along the whole supply chain.

But flow is not all about eliminating waste and reducing inventory and cost, it makes your whole business more agile. With less to move around, it's a whole lot easier to change direction when the market changes or something new emerges from your R&D machine. I hear people talking all the time about Lean and Agile as if they are two different things. In my view they are one and the same thing: you can't be one without the other. I like the Agile term personally, as I think it conveys a better image of what it is all about. However, it's sometimes difficult to get the right message across given the common misconception mentioned above. An explanation I like and that seems to fit well is one that was thought up by Patrick Rigoni, a Founding Partner of SmartChain International, and goes as follows:

> "**True agility** – combines responsiveness with flexibility to deliver flow and is 'designed in' with Lean and Demand Driven Replenishment."

In Figure 1 it's all about finding ways to widen *a)* and shorten *b)*. Notice too that this can apply to anything; here it is just termed *"Operating Parameter"*. This is deliberate as the business requirement should drive what exactly it is that you need to be Agile in: speed to market; delivery to customers; processing claims; getting round the supermarket.

I like this explanation a lot. I remember our team agonising over this for some time, trying to capture the essence of what agility was in relation to Lean in a way that is simple and easy to get your head around – after all, that's the mantra of Lean. Isn't it?

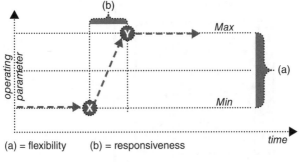

(a) = flexibility   (b) = responsiveness

Figure 1

The secret to maximising flow is to identify the constraint, what's stopping you doing whatever it is, and eliminate it. Not much of a secret really, but it's surprising how difficult this can be when you don't have a good view of the end-to-end supply chain and, on top of that, the pesky thing keeps moving around! More on this later.

Identify and eliminate waste

Before we can start taking steps to eliminate waste, we need to learn how to recognise waste when we see it. To do this we have to come back to our old friend, value. By definition, if what we are doing creates or adds value, as we have defined it above, then what we are doing is not waste. That's fairly simple. Also, by the same token, anything we do that is not adding value is waste. So all we need to do is look around for all the things that are not adding value and stop doing them. Sounds very straightforward, but there is so much of it that it's very easy to get confused and overwhelmed. This is why we categorise waste into seven different types called, funnily enough: "The 7 Wastes". These are shown in Figure 2. In order to further help look for them, they are grouped into what they apply to: people, processes and products or services. This approach has

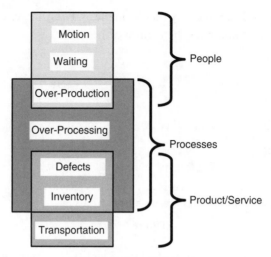

Figure 2 The 7 Wastes

been around for a long time and there are many articles and book chapters on the subject of waste, which define and categorise them far better than I could do here, so while not wanting to skate over such an important subject, I'll encourage you to look up one of the established texts on the subject when you have time, rather than repeat it all here. However, in simple terms, this is what they are, with a brief everyday example included:

Motion – People moving themselves, or parts of themselves, around. Having the fridge, the worktable and the cooker too far apart in the kitchen. Taking the plates from the dishwasher to the cupboard one at a time.

Waiting Time – People waiting for something to arrive or something to happen: Going and standing at the bus stop for 30 minutes when you knew there wasn't a bus due. Waiting for the kettle to boil.

Overproduction – Making more than was needed: The three extra copies of a report you printed just in case a few uninvited people showed up to the meeting. Overfilling the kettle – see Waiting Time above!

Overprocessing – Doing more than is necessary for the purpose: Polishing the underside of the table – no one's going to look! Cutting, then trimming a fence post to exactly 125.25 centimetres.

Defects – Doing something wrong or breaking something: Burning the toast. Making something that's not in compliance with the required specification.

Inventory – Actually should say "excess inventory", products or materials waiting to be used: Car dealership forecourt full of cars for sale. Five cartons of milk in the fridge.

Transportation – The product version of Motion above, products being moved around: Products in trucks moving from the manufacturer to the warehouse or on to the store. Passing the salt around the table at dinner.

It's also worth mentioning that some texts quote a further, eighth waste: the misuse of capacity or resources. My belief is that this is a consequence of the other wastes rather than a waste in its own right, but that's just my opinion.

When looking for waste, you need to be absolutely ruthless, there's no room for sentiment here. If there isn't a clear and direct line of sight to customer value, then it's waste; sorry, but there you are. When you start pointing this out, you are going to become very unpopular very quickly, so it's best to prepare your audience before setting out. As a rule of thumb, 90%+ of everything a business does is waste. If you're not seeing this, then you're either not looking hard enough or you're being too soft. Once you understand this and manage to get your leaders understanding it too, huge improvements in performance are possible. Having said that, not all waste can be eliminated. There are two types to consider. Type 1 waste is that which is associated with doing your business, such as the company accounts or QA testing. While it can't be totally eliminated, you should look for ways to pare it down to the absolute minimum, but recognise that while it is unavoidable, it's still waste. You'll get into some very heated debates with your Head of Quality over this last one, but testing adds no value to the product if it was made properly in the first place – sorry, but there you are! The other, Type 2 waste, usually more than 60% of the total, adds no value whatsoever to anyone and is not required to satisfy any external regulation or need. This waste should be eliminated and the resources used for something more useful.

Sounds simple, but it's not. Persuading a large number of people that the majority of what they do on a day-to-day basis amounts to waste is hard, both for the message giver and the message receiver. Over the years, whole departments have been created to generate and distribute waste, which others use to generate more waste, and so the cycle goes on. At the risk of getting locked up for treason, just look at governments of countries for outstanding examples of this. Breaking this will be one of the hardest things you will have to do, as you will be butting up against company hierarchy and politics.

In this section I will leave you with one final comment on waste. Your most precious commodity is time. Time marches on relentlessly and once gone, you never get it back again. Ensuring time is not wasted must be the number one priority. If you think about it, the implications of this are quite profound. As someone who is getting on a bit now, I really am beginning to understand the meaning of this in every aspect of life.

Declare war on variation

Variation is the killer of Lean processes: it generates so much waste planning for it, trying to quantify it and buffering against it. All of which is treating the symptom, not the cause. This is where our friend, Six Sigma, comes into play. The Six Sigma suite of tools provides a systematic approach to defining, measuring and analysing variability and then designing and implementing changes to reduce and control it. This was codified into a method by Motorola in the

1980s under the acronym DMAIC (Define opportunity area, Measure current performance, Analyse opportunity potential, Improve performance, Control performance). Again, at the risk of sounding evasive, there are many books on the subject written by people far more versed in these tools than me. If you really want the full works on this you can do worse than getting your hands on a copy of one of Michael L. George's books, founder of The George Group. Briefly however, in principle it works like this:

Firstly, identify an area that is not performing well, or where there is a specific problem that needs fixing. This needs to be agreed and sponsored, as there needs to be real commitment to fixing it.

Secondly, spend some time understanding how the area you are trying to improve works and get some real data on performance at each step of the process. It is important that this is done properly as it is the basis of all to come. This means that you need to take the time to get a statistically relevant sample, taking in the true variability of the process.

Thirdly, analyse the data to understand the root causes of the behaviours that the process is exhibiting. It's important not just to focus on the down side; it's just as important to understand the causes of good outcomes so they can be replicated. There is a whole host of tools and models available to do this.

Fourthly, figure out how to improve performance or fix the problem and implement the solution (Ha! That sounds simple doesn't it? In practice it can be far from it).

Fifthly and finally, put measures, controls, accountabilities and fail-safe mechanisms in place to stop everything sliding back to the old ways.

I'm sure there will be many Six Sigma black belts having palpitations and fuming after reading this very brief explanation. If you are one of those, please be assured that I'm in no way trying to downplay the importance or effectiveness of this method for turning around performance. As will be discussed later, Six Sigma and

Lean are good friends and, indeed, should be blended in any broad improvement programme.

Variation can kill the process, but much variation can be eliminated by applying some simple discipline into the way activities are carried out without the need to resort to some of the more powerful tools mentioned above. Empowerment is a much overused buzzword these days and I keep hearing how "everyone needs to be empowered". While this might be true, if not done with a little discipline, all you end up with is a free-for-all and everything gets out of control. If the ways of working are inconsistent, the outcomes will be too. This is a problem for any business, but if you operate in any of the numerous regulated industries, it's a major issue, hence the enormous quality management departments in many of these businesses. There has to be "one right way" for everything. However, if you can't get to the "right" way then at least get to "one way" while you figure out what the "right" way is. This can be as simple as looking around your organisation at all the people doing a particular task and doing a rough evaluation on who does it the best. For production, this is fairly easy as there are probably pretty good measures around. For other tasks, this might be a bit more tricky, but don't sweat it too much, we're only looking for rank, not absolutes, here. Once discovered, get the people from the best group to document how they carry out the task and then teach the rest how to do it. The more difficult issue is then to make sure everyone does it, and sometimes this can involve a real battle against the "not invented here" brigade. Everyone will insist they are different and so-and-so's solution won't work here, but don't be having any of it. If there are differences, get them to prove it; the onus of proof should be on them, not you.

"Ah," I hear you say. "Doesn't all this standardisation stifle innovation, the cornerstone of continuous improvement?" Not really, but continuous improvement needs to be introduced in a controlled way, not randomly. Once the new way is tested and shown to be better, this then becomes the new standard, hence my message above about not necessarily being "right" right off the bat. By way of an example of what I mean here: Imagine the person replacing the left rear wheel in the middle of a Formula One race having a bright idea about how to do it better and then trying it out there and then. Result, a three-wheeled F1 car exiting the pit lane into the barrier at a high rate of knots! No, these guys follow a well-rehearsed process to the letter; everything has to be done exactly to plan with no deviations. But, once back at base, they try out all sorts of stuff to shave 0.1 seconds off the time it takes, but this is done in a development environment, not in "production". Once they find, test and perfect a better way, then this becomes the new standard. This is how F1 wheel changes have steadily reduced from 20+ seconds to fewer than 5 over the years, with a distinct lack of three-wheeled missiles coming out of the pit lane. So, proof positive the standard ways of working and innovation do work very well together.

Organise your people around outcomes you want

Companies over the decades (centuries?) have been organised by departments of people focusing on the same activities: finance; marketing; production; sales; quality; planning, etc. In turn, these departments have usually been sub-divided into groups of people all doing the same thing. The reasons for this are many, including skills development, economies of scale, "centres of excellence" and a myriad of other reasons, but one stands out for me: it's easier to manage a group of people if they all have similar skills and are doing similar work. This also makes it easier to "manage talent" and create career paths and promotion opportunities. So, it seems that the majority of companies are organised for the benefit of the people and managers in them, rather than what they are supposed to be delivering to the customer. In addition, this type of organisation creates a lot of barriers and "handoffs" between these departments, resulting in inevitable delay as your value moves through its process towards the customer, and a lot of finger pointing and bickering when things don't go quite according to plan.

A solution to this is the "process-centric organisation" or PCO structure. Once you have a clear understanding of what you are trying to achieve, you need to organise your people to deliver it. That means pulling teams together with the right skills with good leadership, clear goals and full accountability. A lot of nice words that sound very clever, but what do they really mean? Again, many companies have a terrible time understanding and implementing a process-centric organisation, but in reality, they do it all the time and just don't realise it. Here's how. Give any manager in any organisation a problem to solve, or a change to make, which will require more than casual thinking about over a coffee and they will naturally do the right thing: they will initiate a project. They will ask a few questions about what it is they are being asked to do, set some objectives and targets, sometimes in the form of a project charter, and understand the skills needed to meet the objectives. They will pull a team together with the right skills, appoint a project leader and then leave them to get on with it, but periodically monitor and measure the outcomes to determine whether the team and/or the leader get a bonus or a good kicking. Virtually every business has done this, and most have quite well-defined processes to do it. Let's look at that definition of what a process-centric organisation is again: team of people; right skills; leadership; clear goals and accountability. Aha! Starting to sound quite familiar now isn't it? So a "PCO" is nothing more than a project team, except the project isn't a discrete piece of work with a beginning and end, but the process of delivering the business's products or services to the customer. In essence, that's all there is to it; not that clever, and everyone does it already. So why isn't every business organising itself this way? There are two main reasons for this: firstly, it's not quite as simple as outlined above; this team, the process execution team, can't work in isolation: they need supporting and guiding, which gets people all tied up in knots on how to do it. Secondly, there tends to be a huge dose of history and ego wrapped up in the current hierarchy which gets in the way. There's a whole chapter devoted to this subject, so we'll look at these problems and potential solutions in a bit more detail later.

Equip your people with the right skills

Working in a Lean environment is different; it requires new skills as well as a new way of thinking. The people in your organisation need to understand the processes and the context of their own contribution to it. They need to be able to carry out the tasks they are assigned competently and take a lot more ownership in resolving issues for themselves, or within the team. There is much less reliance on inspection and QC to find and fix problems. Therefore, the skill level, not just in the tasks, but also in problem-solving techniques needs to be at a higher level if problems and errors are to be avoided in this new world. If this is not systematically taken care of at the outset, then quality will suffer and the "all evil" variability will start to raise its ugly head. Both of these issues will result in confidence being lost at all levels in your fledgling Lean program before it really gets off the ground, and will probably end up killing it.

Lean deployment and working in a Lean environment also require a number of tools and techniques to be learned and applied. While at the outset you may tool up a group of people selected from your organisation to learn and use these tools, or, dare I say it, hire some consultants to help you, this situation is not sustainable and you will need a broader spectrum of your organisation's population to be "Lean savvy". They will need to be able to recognise the need and apply appropriate Lean tools as part of their day-to-day work. Again, this education needs to be planned and delivered through classroom sessions for the basics and awareness, but more importantly on-the-job coaching by your "experts". Also, don't expect this to happen overnight. After all, you don't give someone a musical instrument, show them how it works and give them a lesson, then expect them to deliver a faultless solo performance at the Albert Hall, do you?

Clear and simple measures and controls

According to Peter Drucker, "what gets measured gets done".

In my experience this is one of the most accurate statements made in business folklore. If something is being measured then it gives the impression, rightly or wrongly, that someone in management is interested in it and is monitoring whether the responsible party is actually doing it. This is usually a good enough incentive for that particular responsible party to do whatever needs to be done to make that particular measurement indicate that enough is being done to prevent a kicking from the boss, or maybe even a bonus.

So, in our Lean world, as long as we measure everything that could possibly influence the delivery of value to our customers, everything will get done and everyone lives happily ever after, right? Well, in theory, maybe. In reality, having a very concise set of critical measures that is clear and drives the right actions is the key to success. Sounds simple, but in practice it is sometimes very hard to do. We will cover specific measures to help you manage a Lean business in a later chapter, but now let's look at the types that exist and how they can be used.

Measures fall into two categories: lagging and leading, also known as outcome and causal. The first one only has value in reporting what has happened and cannot be changed; it is looking at the past. Apart from being able to tell a good or bad story about how you have done, lagging measures are of little value to managing your business. It's like stepping on the scales when you are trying to lose weight: it tells you whether you have been good or naughty with the cream cakes last week, but does not tell you if you are going to be lighter next week.

The other guys, leading or causal, are much more use to you, they help you manage your activities and can provide the basis to predict the outcome before it happens. In our weight loss analogy, leading measures would be calorie counting and exercise logging: eat less and work out more and you can predict what the scales will say at the end of the week. So, if we take care of the leaders, the laggers will take care of themselves.

In summary, your measures need to enable you to answer the following questions:

* Are you delivering enough stuff?
* Are you delivering the right stuff? See above to determine what the right stuff is!
* Are you producing the minimal amount of waste?

Every business will need a slightly different set of measures to answer these questions, but we will explore some of the more common ones and some of the best practices later.

There is another set of measures or, more correctly, controls I have to mention here. Again, there will be more of this later, so this is just a brief introduction. These are the early warning indicators and visual controls.

These are located at the "sharp end" in the midst of the action. They provide real-time feedback on what is going on and let you know if you're going to have a good day or if a potential issue is brewing before it happens. If possible the controls should be very visual, without the need to run a report: simple boards and charts filled in by the people who actually do the work, because they can do this task better. As a general rule on visual controls, consider the following:

> Anyone should be able to determine the current health of the operation by standing in the middle of the area and looking around. It should be immediately obvious where attention is needed without asking anyone.

Next chance you get, take a trip down to the action and have a look around your operation. If you're honest, can you see what's really going on?

Defining your "Ideal State"

Now you have some of the basic concepts understood, you need to interpret them in the context of your business and knock that fictional grinning cat on the head. You need to apply these simple principles to set a very clear ambition for your business. Ask yourself the question: "How could this business look and feel in 5–7 years' time if we removed all the barriers to change and applied these principles to the full?" Don't let the "Ah yes but" brigade stop you. Be bold and aim high – only by doing this will the real questions and issues you need to address come to the surface. Why 5–7 years? Because this time frame is close enough not to be pure "blue sky" fantasy, but far enough out to avoid the baggage of the here and now constraining your thinking. I've been into many companies and asked if they have a clear picture of the future and been answered with a bland wordy PowerPoint slide about being an "upper quartile, customer-centric, learning organisation" and other such phrases which could, and indeed should, apply to just about any company on the planet. And before we move on, what's all this "upper quartile" stuff all about? Does an Olympic athlete train like crazy for four years to go to the games to be "upper quartile"? No, they go there to win, to be number one, and so should your business. Going in with an ambition that up to 24% of your competitors will beat you to a pulp is the wrong attitude in my mind.

Anyway, enough venting on my part. So, what we are looking for here is something far more concrete – a clear definition of the look and feel of your company from all angles: the way your products and services flow to the customer; the information needed to support that flow; the way you will structure your organisation around it; the required skills and behaviours you expect in order to be successful. It's all about *your* business, *your* people and how *you* intend to operate, not something vanilla which could apply to anyone.

It does not matter how you do this, but it had better be clear, compelling and relevant to everyone involved with your business, including your customers and suppliers, if you are going to get them all energised around getting there in the next 2–3 years.

Hold on! 2–3 years? It was 5–7 a paragraph ago. Is there something devious going on here or have I just lost it? Well, despite popular belief, I haven't quite lost it just yet. The 5–7 years was a bit of a fib just to get people thinking the right way. Once you have the plot mapped out, usually there is no real reason why any business can't achieve its Ideal State in 2–3 years. This starts to instil a sense of urgency, which will be needed later to maintain the progress.

A nice flash paper or presentation on your future that gets discussed once in a high power meeting and then never sees the light of day again won't cut it either. You need to get everyone on board. Firstly get the leaders engaged and in agreement; then they have to engage the rest of the organisation, putting the case and the picture into context for each and every person.

In conclusion

So, those are the basic concepts and the first step in understanding the journey you are about to embark on. As you can see, I have devoted much of the precious space in this book to the "people" elements. That's because these are more difficult to implement and more critical to get right. As a colleague at another company once said at a conference Q&A session on Lean: "I can change processes and equipment quickly and easily, if I'm given enough money. But no matter how much money I have, I can't change people's behaviours and skills quickly or easily." These human factors of Lean are the difference between making long-lasting change in a business and merely cost cutting, which can only ever be a short-term fix to buy you time; a little more on this later when we talk about business cases for change.

I'll close this chapter in the same way I closed the last one. None of this will work if it all ends up just being words on a slide or talk in a Ra-Ra session by the management team. If any of this is going to be of any use at all, there must be discipline demonstrated by everyone to live by the rules. When temptation beckons, remember emptying the fridge into the waste bin!

If you are really strapped for time and only feel you need a quick dip into Lean, you could stop here, but I encourage you at least to skim through the rest of the chapters and read a bit more thoroughly the ones relevant to you before putting this book down. For those wanting more, read on! The next few chapters dig into some of these areas a little more.

3

MORE ABOUT FLOW

We introduced flow and the importance of good, predictable flow to efficiency in the last chapter. This is such an important subject and so fundamental that it deserves a chapter to itself. Having said this, why is flow so important?

Flow is about keeping everything moving at a steady pace through the process from start to finish. Notice I say here "steady pace", not as fast as possible. That's not to say that you shouldn't accelerate the pace if you can, but the important thing is getting everything moving at the same pace from beginning to end. If you can achieve this, a number of quite remarkable things start to happen.

With consistency comes reliability. It is much easier to predict the outcome, which means that when you say to your customers "we can do this by next Tuesday morning", there is a much better likelihood that come Tuesday morning it will have arrived; in other words, good service. Another aspect of consistency is that quality also tends to improve. Now that's a nice bonus, as the cost of poor quality is huge in most industries.

To build a bit more on the above, although the emphasis is not on speed, good flow does have a habit of getting things through faster. So, before flow, your answer to a customer would more likely be "we can do this in three weeks", and even with this answer you would probably have your fingers crossed behind your back. Now, with faster, more reliable service and improved quality, three weeks becomes two or even one week with no crossed fingers. This all means happier customers and, guess what, you're likely to sell more, so revenue goes up. Yeehaa! High fives all round for flow!

Flow also means that stuff does not get snarled up in the works, so there is a lot less "stuff" in the pipe. All this "stuff" hoards money, in people's time and in materials, which has now made it out to the customer who will have paid for it. As a result, there is a lot more cash in the bank even though we haven't sold any more. And while we're on the subject, if there's less "stuff" in the process, it takes a lot less effort to manage it, so costs tend to go down too. More high fives!

OK, so given this very brief case for flow, it looks like it gets most people's vote for being quite important. Now we understand this, let's look at how to get it.

Maintaining a steady flow is all about maintaining the balance between demand and capacity at all times. If you have flexibility in your capacity at all points along the way, then achieving this is simple and you just let nature take its course. Actually, that's quite a good analogy – let's look deeper. Take a river flowing down a valley, for instance. This is a perfect example of what I'm talking about: whatever the conditions, the water keeps going on its journey to the sea. If there's more water, because there's been some rain, the river gets a bit deeper or wider and the flow continues. If the valley gets narrower, or there are rocks in the way, the water builds up a bit behind it, the pressure increases and pushes the water through a little faster to compensate, again, maintaining the balance. So, nature has a smart way of dealing with this. It is not surprising really, as the laws of physics and 14 billion years of history have all played a part in it.

How, then, do we mere mortals replicate this state of affairs in our businesses and everyday life?

Know your limitations (aka constraints)

This is the first, and a very important, step. The primary key here, as hinted above, is identifying and relieving the constraint. This is the heart of the "Theory of Constraints" on which there have been numerous books and literally hundreds of articles written. The most well known is probably *The Goal*, by Dr Eliyahu Goldratt who started it all. The following is a brief introduction to the core principles of the theory.

The constraint is the part of the process which governs the pace or capacity of the whole. In a lot of cases, this is obvious, but in others it is not quite so simple, particularly in cases where there are different things going on at different times and you have a programme of continuous improvement on the go as well. However, let's not get ahead of ourselves and make things too complicated just yet. So, in a simple situation, how do you go about locating the constraint?

Let's go back to our river analogy. What tends to happen when there is something in the way of the river flow is that water starts to build up ahead of it, forming a lake or just a wider section of slower-moving water. This is exactly what happens in your process flows. So, one way to identify the constraint is to look for lakes, or for where the work is piling up waiting to be worked on. This could be pallets in front of a machine, or simply an overfull inbox of unread messages. Either way, this means that stuff is arriving faster than it can be processed before the next lot arrives and you've found the constraint.

There are other clues to identifying the constraint. For instance, where the highest utilisation rate is, or where all the expediting goes on, but probably the most reliable method is to ask the people working the process. They are working in the thick of it all day and every day and usually know exactly where the bottlenecks and problems are by instinct.

Notice that throughout this whole section I've used the words "the constraint" not "a constraint". This is important as there is a very clear rule at play here. In any one situation, there is only one constraint governing the overall rate of flow through the system. It can move as things change, but in any single situation there can only be one.

In order to check if you've found it, you need to look at how things are moving either side of it. Upstream, to keep with the river analogy, you will probably find the flow rate over time is a bit lumpy as things react to changes in pressure or demand. Immediately downstream, you will probably find the flow is smoother as the constraint lops off the peaks and fills in the troughs. So, if you see both a pile of stuff and a change in the flow characteristics, you can be fairly confident that you've found it.

Now you've found it, what do you do with it? There are only two things you can do really:

1. Get some more.
2. Ensure it keeps working.

OK, so of these two options, which do you pick? The first is quite simple, but usually a bit expensive so should be a last resort if all else fails. However, before wasting a lot of time trying to solve using the second, it is important to do a simple test, as outlined below.

First, find out what the true capacity of your constraint is over an extended period. Unfortunately, this is not necessarily what it says on the label, as this is usually a theoretical maximum which will probably bear no relation to what is possible in your situation. You need to look back over time and calculate the demonstrated average capacity. Next you need to check what the average demand is over a recent period of time. If the first is bigger than the second, then method 2 should sort out the problem. If the second is bigger than the first, you have a more fundamental problem and you just need to go get some more capacity, be it through buying another piece of equipment, hiring more people or increasing the number of hours available to work. This is quite easy to test really, because if there is indeed a deficiency in the latent capacity, the build-up in front of the constraint will keep growing.

Once you've figured out that, on average, you are OK, then the next thing to do is employ a few tricks to keep things moving. The key thing here is to avoid as much downtime as possible, which means three things: taking good care of it so it doesn't break; keeping it well fed with work to do; and reducing stoppages to a minimum. This last one has a sting in the tail for Lean, so we'll cover this one at the end.

Take good care of your constraint

Sounds totally obvious in theory but can be surprisingly difficult in practice. Taking care means making sure that you keep it well maintained and don't push it beyond its design limits; again, totally obvious, so what's the problem? The problem is that since we are talking about the constraint, that is the very thing that governs the overall output from the process, there is huge pressure not to stop the constraint and push it to the limit and beyond to get the absolute maximum out of it. The number of arguments I've heard, and been involved in, where the engineering crew want to take the machine down for maintenance only to be confronted with an irate production manager screaming to be heard over the noise of screeching metal-on-metal sounds: "Have you seen the backlog here, and you want me to stop for the rest of the day for you to tinker with it, are you insane?". Unfortunately, the end result is usually a good day's production run followed by a disaster a few days later when something terminal happens to the machine. As the subject of all this commotion is the constraint, stopping it for maintenance is always a touchy subject, but necessary in the long run. The key to success and avoiding some bruises here is good planning and setting expectations well in advance.

Feed meeeeeee!!!

This is all about making sure that the constraint keeps working. This is usually done by keeping a buffer of work ahead of the constraint so that if the supply dries up for whatever reason, the constraint doesn't have to stop as a result, throwing away precious capacity. This is a whole lot more than just piling up as much stuff as possible and hoping for the best, there is maths at play here. The size of the buffer will depend on a number of dynamic factors that need to be understood and quantified if it's going to work properly. These factors are:

- The overall average load or throughput required (Tr). Don't forget that this should be as required by the customer. Remember the first principle in Chapter 1?
- The demonstrated throughput of the constraint when it is working properly (Td). This is important, as this governs the potential of the constraint to "catch up" after a period of downtime.
- The supply variability (V). This is the difficult one. What this really means is when the constraint has an unplanned stop, how long does it take to get it up and running again on average, and how variable is it? This is sometimes quite difficult to determine, as very often there is a dearth of reliable data on this and you will be stuck with anecdotal evidence only. No matter, if in doubt err on the pessimistic side.
- Finally, the acceptable "failure to comply" rate (S). What this means is how often will you accept that all the stars are against you and your constraint has run out of work and has to stop? You can't cover for every eventuality as you would need to build a new warehouse just to hold the buffer!

Once you have this information, you can calculate the size of the buffer needed to keep the constraint fed under normal situations, accepting that you can't cover for all eventualities. The simple approach to this is:

1. Work out your average demand, per day, per hour, whatever.
2. Work out how long it takes to get a batch of new supply to the constraint (in the same units as used above).

3. Multiply the above two numbers together. This is the lead time component.
4. Find out what the minimum batch size is for supply. Note this is not necessarily the batch size for the constraint.
5. Add this to the number in step 3.
6. Now, talk to a few people and get some idea of the variability of the demand on the constraint and the variability of the supply. If the answer is "high" in both cases, be safe and add 100% of the number in step 3; if the answer is "medium" or "high and low", add 50% of the number in step 3; if the answer is "low" in both cases, add 30%. This part takes care of the uncertainties in the supply process and what you need to get out of the constraint.

Now, at this point, all the statisticians among you will be throwing your arms up in horror at this gross simplification but we are talking practical application not academic exactness. The truth of the matter is that the real world is not exact, and as long as you are roughly right and not completely wrong you will be OK. The above errs on the safe side, so if it is a bit out and you end up with a bigger pile ahead of the constraint than you need, you can always tweak it down a bit later.

Keeping going

Given the subject above, this seems at odds with the message provided in the first section, but it's not really. This is about making sure that you are optimising the way you use the constraint and avoiding unnecessary downtime. Things to think about here are:

- Sequencing the order of products you need to produce. In a lot of cases there are big differences in the time it takes to change from one product to another, depending on the degree of difference between the products. Paint mixing is an obvious example; there is an optimal colour change sequence to minimise the amount of cleaning required as you progress from white to black and back again. Having the buffer in place helps here, as you now have the ability to do some optimisation without forcing the rest of the process to conform to your sequence.

- Fast changeovers, figuring out how to move from one product to the next in the shortest possible time reliably. Remember the F1 pit stop story in Chapter 2? This is what I'm talking about. Any change over reduction effort should be targeted at the constraint first. This has much wider implications for Lean in terms of being able to respond quicker to changes and shortening lead times as well. If there is a silver bullet for Lean, this might well be it.

- Constant monitoring. Don't leave the constraint to its own devices for long. If it's that important, have someone there to keep an eye on it, even if they don't need to be doing something to it all the time. Murphy's Law says that as soon as you turn your back, something will go wrong and you can't afford for this to happen at the constraint.

- Finally, when things do go bang, and they will, have a well-oiled and available response in place to deal with it as quickly as possible. Fixing the broken constraint has to be the number one priority, even if it means dropping something else.

If you follow these simple guidelines, you should be able to keep things moving and cut yourself a little slack. You might even be able to avoid a big capital expense in the process and become a real hero!

The Whack-a-Mole game of constraints

Yep, you read right – the arcade game where the moles pop out of their burrows at random and you have to whack them before they pop back in again. Constraints have a nasty habit of moving around and popping up somewhere else, just when and where you least expected them. In this section, we'll look at the possible reasons for this and explore a few ways of dealing with them.

The dish of the day is...

In most cases businesses don't do or make one thing, and in today's world and into the future, your markets are, and will be, demanding more and more diversity from you to secure their custom. As a result, your people and equipment have to deal with a range of tasks that put differing loads on them, depending on what it is that they are making that day.

As a consequence, what might be the constraint for one product or service might not be for another. An example of this in one of my stomping grounds, the pharmaceutical industry, is in tablet manufacture. Making a "pill" requires many different steps: blending, granulation, milling, compression, coating and so on. These steps can take differing lengths of time dependent on the particular content, size and shape of the pill. Given that in most cases the capacity of the equipment is fairly closely matched – on average, the constraint in the end-to-end process will move from step to step, depending on the mix of the products needed to be made. This is not usually a problem in the short term, but if there is a trend in the market which changes the underlying mix of products, then the constraint will move to another point in the process.

And our latest offering is...

This one is closely related to the example above, but instead of being a gradual shift comes as a result of a specific event, a new product launch or a radical change in the way a product or service is processed. Typically, new products have different characteristics and place different demands on the capacity used to produce them. In addition, in many cases the new product or service replaces an existing one, so the impact can be doubled.

Entropy

Next there's good old entropy, the relentless passage of time which eventually grinds everything to dust. As parts of your process get older, their capabilities change and things start to slow down or break down more often. Ah yes, you say, but isn't that what maintenance is for? True, but no matter how hard you try, you can't completely beat nature. If this happened at the same rate everywhere, this wouldn't be a problem; it would only impact the overall capacity not where the constraint is. But, as usual, life just doesn't play ball fairly and this rate of decay varies from place to place. If your constraint is decaying at a slower rate than somewhere else, then eventually the capacity lines will cross and, hey presto! Your constraint has moved somewhere else.

Continuous improvement

This is the really unfair one, but sits at the heart of any Lean programme. The whole point of this chapter is to explain the importance the constraint has on the performance of the whole and to make sure that improvement efforts are focused here, where they will do the most good. So you do this. Everyone busts a gut to improve the constraint and after all the effort – SUCCESS! You've increased effective capacity by 25% and the party begins. Then a few days later, someone bursts the bubble by showing the latest results and somehow, after all that effort, it's still not working as it should. The problem is that you've improved the capability of the constraint to such an extent that the pinch point has moved somewhere else. No matter, you cry: "Forward to the next challenge!" and everyone rallies round and starts tackling the new bad boy. This is all great stuff; however, there is a problem, which in the enthusiasm to move on to the next challenge can get forgotten about. In the traditional world, the impact of this is not too bad, but in a Lean world, the results can be a major problem. By way of an example, let me tell a short story of a particular case of this, and then we can explore why this happened and what to do about it. That is if you haven't worked it out already.

A few years ago, we were working with a client to implement Lean processes throughout their manufacturing plants worldwide. One site in particular really got the bug and threw everything they had at it, with remarkable results. Service levels went through the roof, lead time tumbled from 29 days to just 8 days; costs went down; and stress levels at the site from operators to the site leader went down 3 or 4 notches as everything just ran much more smoothly. However, they didn't stop there. They applied all the new thinking to their continuous improvement effort and did a remarkable job at the constraint. Again, there was much jubilation and credit from the bosses at corporate headquarters and everyone started looking for the next place to tackle. Then it all started to unravel. The first symptoms appeared on the shop floor. What was once a smooth-running operation requiring minimal intervention to work like clockwork started to need much more attention to make sure flow was maintained. Work in progress started to build up in odd places and, while things were better than before, it just seemed like hard work to keep things on track. Eventually, the site key performance indicators (KPIs) started to suffer and that's when the real questions started to be asked in high places. So what happened? We were called back to take a look and explain why things were going wrong and it immediately became apparent that the constraint had moved. This was no real surprise to anyone, but what they had missed was that in a Lean world, processes are designed end to end to best manage the constraint, and if this moves, then the whole set-up is now off balance. It was this imbalance that was causing all the problems, as they were now forcing the process to work, rather than the process working automatically.

The fix wasn't too difficult in reality and they managed to do it themselves using the tools they had learned the first time around. All it took was a change in the buffer position and a new sequencing calculation at the new constraint and, within a few weeks, everything was running smoothly again.

And the moral of all this...

The bottom line here is that the world changes and you have to change with it. If you don't, you'll get caught out like our friends above. This is a lot more important in a Lean world because, as everything is much more finely tuned, there's a lot less slack in the system. Designing the new world is not a one-time-then-forget exercise. When something changes or you see the outcomes starting to wander off what you were expecting, it's a signal to do a "Renewal". We'll talk about this in a later chapter in more depth, but what this means in summary is that you need to take a look at all the parameters of your design and check to make sure they are all still valid. This includes: buffer levels; buffer and trigger positions; production sequencing; and minimum batch sizes, to name but a few. Don't get too alarmed: this is not as onerous as it sounds and not everything needs to be done every time.

Some everyday examples of flow – or the lack of it!

In keeping with the principles of this book, let's try and put a little everyday context on all this. Let's look at a few typical, and in a lot of cases, frustrating, situations that most of us have been in at some time, which demonstrate what we are talking about here.

Traffic lights vs. roundabouts

As should be obvious by now, flow is all about keeping things moving. If you can, avoid stopping, or at least if something has to stop, it shouldn't hold everything else up. The problem of keeping traffic flowing on the roads has been an ever-increasing problem since the horse and cart, but became a major issue with the mass availability of motor transport for individuals. While there are always temporary hold-ups and constrictions that slow things down, by far and away the biggest issues to traffic flow occur when two major roads cross each other. While there are a few ways to deal with this, the most common two are roundabouts (rotations or circles if you are in North America) and traffic lights. Let's look at how these work to keep flow going, and the pitfalls of each.

Traffic lights

OK, no need to explain how these work (however, the light sequence and timing are different between Europe and North America, which can catch you out if you're not used to it – reference a £60 fine and three points for jumping a red light after returning to the UK from living in the US a while back!). From a flow perspective this solution is not really that good. Let's pick this apart a bit to explain what I mean.

Traffic lights work by stopping one flow to let another start, then swapping over after a period of time. This means at any one time, one side is stopped. While it's stopped, traffic is queuing up waiting for the green light. When the green finally comes, there is a delay from when the light changes to when the first car starts to move and this delay cascades and builds down the line. If you've ever sat in a line waiting for green and the pesky thing has turned red again before you even start to move, you know what I mean here. This delay is building in inefficiency and reducing the effective capacity of the intersection at peak times. This is why there are always hold-ups at traffic lights when it's busy.

In addition, there is a practical minimal time for a signal to stay green. As a result of this, when traffic is light, you can be sitting at a red light when all the roads are completely clear. Very frustrating, especially when you're late! I know most have variable timers and sensors, but still, traffic lights artificially interrupt flow rather than letting natural constraints manage it automatically.

Roundabouts

These are the essence of a Lean solution. Everything is open for use at all times; all a driver needs to do is check to make sure they are not going to collide with something already on the roundabout. If there's nothing there, keep going, as there are no predetermined stop and go times as there are with the lights. A few simple rules to follow, after that, use some common sense. This approach minimises the interruption to the flow and as long as the demand doesn't exceed the capacity, everything keeps moving.

However, as usual when something simple has been working fine for decades, someone has to start messing with it. In recent years, the ever-increasing volume of traffic has started to push things to the limits. Traffic lights started appearing on roundabouts in an attempt to stop traffic building up on the approach to a roundabout, because one dominant road hogged all the capacity and there was never a big enough gap for someone coming in from another road to get on. If you consider the pros and cons outlined above, this is the daftest idea possible. Think about it: you build a roundabout to avoid the traffic having to stop unnecessarily and maximise the capacity of an intersection by lowering the batch size of traffic entering and leaving. Then, in someone's infinite wisdom, sets of traffic lights appear on the approach roads, which batches everything up again. Add to this that these "temporary" traffic lights now seem to be on all the time and it only adds to the madness. I can't tell you how many times I've been sitting at a red light at 1:00 a.m., tired and wanting to get home, waiting to get onto an empty roundabout. As I say, madness, but enough of my ranting – let's look a little more calmly at the problem.

The real problem here is not the imbalance of traffic from one side, or even the volume of traffic; it's the speed of the traffic on the roundabout. As roundabouts have got bigger, the speed of the cars on the roundabout has increased. As the speed increases, the size of the gap needed for someone to get onto the roundabout from another road increases, so there are fewer safe opportunities for people waiting to get on. Result: backed-up traffic on the non-dominant approach roads. The solution then is somehow to slow the traffic down, but not stop it completely; then a big enough gap will present itself more often, and things will start to balance themselves out again. Smaller roundabouts, chicanes on the approaches, whatever. In really peak times, traffic lights might still be needed.

The DIY enthusiast

I know I'm a major culprit here. Every day I have to walk into the house and see, with a grimace and an embarrassed smile, the endless array of half-finished DIY jobs. They all started out with good intentions and a clear vision of what the finished result was going to be. The problem is, I didn't apply the famous rule of a certain Icelandic quiz show host: "I've started so I'll finish." For those not familiar with the long-running UK quiz show *Mastermind*, here's a very quick synopsis to put the reference into context. It's a rather highbrow contest where contenders pit their wits against each other in two rounds of rapid-fire specialist subject and general knowledge questions. Each round is two and a half minutes and ends on a buzzer. The rule is that if the questioner had started asking a question when the buzzer sounded, the contender will hear the rest of the question and can attempt an answer. The original host, Magnus Magnusson, attained fame and almost cult status by informing the contender if his question was interrupted by the buzzer, "I've started so I'll finish", before continuing.

All very interesting, but what has this to do with Lean and flow? Well, think about it. Why do you think all those DIY jobs got started but never finished? Apart from the "I got bored and lost interest" ones, most were due either to having too many things on the go at one time, or not making sure that I had everything I needed to finish the job before I started. The constant distractions, having to wait to get the missing stuff and changing priorities all result in a logjam of half-finished jobs and the ones that do get finished take months instead of a couple of days. In Lean words, poor flow.

So, what's the solution to this problem? It's really quite simple, as most Lean things are:

1. Be honest with yourself. Are you really up to doing the job?
2. Are you sure you have the time, with all the other things on your plate, and do you really understand how much time is actually needed to do the job?

If the answer to either of the above two questions is "No", then you shouldn't even start the job or you should call in someone more qualified to do it, or at least to give you a hand.

3. Be a good Scout and heed the Scout's motto: Be Prepared. Make sure you know exactly what you need to finish the job and make sure you have it all before you start. Check, double check, then check again for good measure; even so, you'll probably still forget something, so find out if the shops will be open.

   Also, develop a plan for doing it. This doesn't need to be a 500-line Microsoft Project plan detailing to a microsecond each arm movement and blink, but at least you have an outline of the steps involved. If it's something that has instructions, read them. I know this is not something a certain part of the population likes doing, but swallow the ego a bit and at least take a look.
4. Clear the decks. If the job is messy, make sure things that don't like getting messy are out of the way. If it's big, make sure you

have cleared enough space to avoid knocking over and breaking one of your partner's prized possessions.

5. Finally, employ the aforementioned Icelandic gentleman's rule.

If you're reading this paragraph it means that you have not thrown this book away in disgust with the words, "Does this guy think I'm an idiot" on your lips. That's good, as I had no intention of insulting your intelligence. So now, let's draw the parallels with the business world.

Numbers 1 and 2 above are about making sure that you have the capacity to take on the work and the people doing it are properly trained and available to do it. Again, sounds like stating the obvious, but it's amazing how often I've heard people committing to deliver something with no real idea if it's possible to do that and meet all the other similar commitments they've made to other people.

Number 3 is doing a material check and staging prior to committing people to starting. A word of caution here: a material check is exactly that. Are all the materials and tools needed available now, not on a promise from the supplier for tomorrow morning, but right now? Can you put your hand on it all and are you sure it hasn't been earmarked for something else? If the answer to this is "yes" and "no it hasn't", then collect it all, label it as allocated to your job and take it to the location where the job is going to be done.

Number 4 is all about applying a bit of good old 5S (more on this later) – make sure the work area is set up properly and everything is in place.

Number 5 is, well, number 5. Seriously though, this is the most difficult part. It takes a lot of discipline to stay focused and not get distracted by all the other things going on and keep all the energy concentrated on finishing the job at hand. Very few companies manage this; the evidence is all around you: it's called work in progress (WIP). Other clear indicators that all is not as it should be in this department are long lead times and – the mother of all demons – the dreaded expedite list.

The airport check-in

Finally to my number one gripe, the airport check-in. Being in a job that requires me to do a lot of flying around, I get to experience the delights of this more than most and it never ceases to amaze me, and frustrate me, as to how inefficient this whole process is. So let's take a quick look at it and figure out a few improvements on the way.

In reality the underlying issues are quite simple and boil down to two things:

1. An imbalance between demand and capacity.
2. An ineffective way of dealing with the "problem passenger", which of course is never you is it? (!)

Let's take a look at the first one. The problem here is not one of overall capacity, as I'm sure if you do the maths, it will show that if you take the average check-in time, multiply by the total number of passengers and divide by the number of check-in desks available, you will come out with an answer that says you're fine – on average. However, the demand isn't nice and smooth. Air travel is a classic batch process. For instance, 200 people arrive, 200 people check in or leave bags, 200 people board, and finally, 200 people fly off to their dream holiday in the sun. After that, nothing happens until the next lot starts to arrive and it all starts over. A typical feast or famine situation.

So to avoid the disgruntled passengers, the answer here is to ensure you have enough capacity, right? Sounds simple, but not easy. Having enough people to deal with the peaks, then having them sitting around twiddling their thumbs between the bursts of activity is very inefficient, not to say costly, when the airlines are already in trouble. What's needed is variable capacity, people in reserve to call in when the heat's on, but able to go and do something else in the slack times. Again, not always easy unless you're going to find a load of "busy work" for them to do, which kind of goes against the whole

Lean idea of demand-driven and waste elimination. One solution is sharing with your neighbours. As long as the peaks don't coincide, you can borrow a few people from next door when you're busy and they're not and vice versa. It's this idea that has led to airport service companies springing up recently that provide this flexing capability to all the airlines at the airport. By aggregating the demand across all the airlines, the demand profile throughout the day tends to flatten out, making the capacity to demand balancing a bit easier, not perfect but better. In your company this same effect can be achieved through cross training and flexible job roles, allowing people to go where the work is, rather than what the job description says. This does require a bit of an organisational rethink, but more of this in another chapter.

Ah yes, now we come to the "problem passenger", you know who I mean. It's the person who has turned up late, or has overweight bags, or wants to change something, or.... We've all been there, waiting in line watching the relentless passage of time marching ever closer to your boarding time, wondering what on earth is taking so long. What happens is that you get a couple of these at the open desks and they hold up the staff for ages trying to sort out their problems. Now, the others are overloaded and the queues start to build as there is a constriction on the flow. This is more difficult to deal with as it is very unpredictable. To me the solution is to be brutal. If you have "problem passengers" you need a "problem desk" to deal with them. As soon as an issue presents itself, the person gets directed to the "problem desk" to resolve the issue. Once out of the way, normal flow resumes at all the other desks. Of course, if there aren't any problems, the "problem desk" can deal with others too. What this means is that, now, the constriction is more predictable and limited irrespective of the number of problems that present themselves. If there are a lot of problems, the wait to get them resolved could be very long, of course, which will make those impacted very upset. So, the question to answer is: Do you want everybody somewhat disgruntled, or a few very unhappy and the rest fine? Your call.

By the way, these ideas can be applied equally to anywhere there is a queue: post offices, supermarket check-outs, you name it. Some have started to do this kind of thing already, but there are a few more tricks that could be played to make all our lives a little less stressful.

In conclusion

If you've got this far, you've probably figured out that understanding flow and managing it is at the heart of Lean. While simple in concept, getting to grips with it and then keeping hold of it can sometimes be a bit difficult. However, once you do get a grip and refuse to let go, the results can be staggering. So, in summary, flow is all about:

- Understanding where the constraint is and making sure you keep track of it.
- Defining your buffers and sequencing to manage the flow through the constraint.
- Reviewing the design on a periodic basis and when something significant changes, and adjusting accordingly.

4

LEAN ENTERPRISE VS. LEAN MANUFACTURING

As promised in Chapter 2, I've come back to say a few words about the difference between Lean Enterprise and Lean Manufacturing. So far in this book we have focused on the application of some of the Lean tools and techniques to specific areas of life, both in a business world and in the "real" world. This is all well and good and should make life a little better and simpler, but will it really change the game? I hinted at this one a few times so the answer shouldn't come as a big surprise to anyone: no, it won't; working with one part of a dependent system will usually yield less than stellar results overall. This is the difference between Lean Enterprise and Lean Manufacturing: Lean Manufacturing takes a view of part of the business, while Lean Enterprise takes account of the whole. Don't get me wrong, there is nothing wrong with applying Lean Manufacturing and focusing on the production processes if that is where the main issues are or you are starting out and learning some of the tools and techniques. However, be aware that there is a bigger picture to take account of if the full opportunity is to be realised. In this chapter we will explore a little of what this bigger picture is and attempt to introduce how the parts contribute to the whole. I'm not going to treat each one with equal emphasis as there just isn't the space to do all full justice, but I will major on the more important areas.

Planning vs. execution

We'll start with the core of any business: getting prepared, and then making the decision to act. In other words: planning and execution. Up to now we have focused on "doing stuff" efficiently and effectively, but this is only part of the story. Making sure that you have the right materials, people and equipment in place to do the right stuff at the right time takes planning, and a Lean environment is no exception to this. Indeed, in a Lean world where there is considerably less "slack" in the system, planning becomes even more important as there is less room for the "oopses".

The starting point is the Sales Forecast. There are many ways in which this is put together – here are a few: a statistical prediction based on past history; expected financial budgets translated into sales volumes; a prediction by the sales organisation of what they are going to sell where. To be honest, in a lot of companies, the last one has more than a passing resemblance to the second! In reality though, the forecast is usually a blend of all of the above. This all gets translated into a quantity of specific requirements each month over the next 12–18 months, or longer. If everything were that simple, knowing what to make or buy would be as simple as ordering what the forecast indicated, but, as usual, real life just ain't that simple!

Most products aren't made, and neither are services provided, in a single step. Nearly all require something that needs to be bought or made before being converted into the finished product: a list of such requirements is called a bill of materials (BoM). Therefore, the forecast is matched against the bill of materials for each product and the requirements for all of these are calculated. Service industries also have bills of materials – it is not all about manufacturing. In these industries, it is more about people resources than materials, but there are outsourced services and consumables too. For example, there are a lot of steps and many things that have to come together to successfully process an insurance claim.

In addition, things can't be made, nor services and materials bought, at a moment's notice. The time to make the finished products and buy all the required stuff is taken into account as well. All of this generates a time-phased listing of everything that needs to be done to get the products out to the customer when they are needed. However, there might be some products in the warehouse already or in process and materials in stock or on order that need to be netted off this list.

Now we have a good plan of what is needed when and, more importantly, what needs to be started or ordered when. This is the production and purchasing schedule, which is usually issued on a weekly basis to initiate production or place orders for materials. Because people tend to like a forward view of things, this schedule is usually created a few weeks in advance; this is called the firm period, when everything is locked down.

At some point along the way, the available capacity is looked at and some prioritisation decisions are made if there is a problem.

All the above sounds quite logical doesn't it? Indeed, this is how most Material Requirements Planning (MRP) systems work, albeit a very simplified view. However, let's translate this into everyday terms and see if it still makes sense.

- Let's start off by asking a few people to do some crystal ball gazing and come up with a guess at what's needed. Oh, by the way, they are measured on what they sell, so isn't that likely to influence the guess somewhat?
- Then take this guess and use the material list to figure out what that means in terms of what we might need. We'll also use some out-of-date data on how long it takes to make or buy what we might need. These data are based on averages and standards that very often don't bear much resemblance to the real time it takes. We'll also add in some minimum order quantities created by people who are measured on the efficiency of their part of the chain,

which usually translates into big batches, as you get better unit costs.

- We'll take a look at what we've got already, then go out and buy or make all the stuff we think we might need to be ready for the customer at exactly the right time to satisfy the guess we made in the first place.

Hmm... Doesn't sound quite so great now, does it? OK, this is a rather dim view of what really happens and there is a bit more science involved than I've portrayed here, but in essence this is what happens. Is it any wonder, then, that the result is too much of what you don't need, and not enough of what you do? Add to this all the fire-fighting and finger pointing to try to rescue the situation before the customer starts complaining too much. Adding more fuel to the fire, the MRP system begins to react to the differences and starts sending exception messages and changed requirements every day, amplifying the noise created by the errors in the forecast. As a result, a familiar scene of chaos starts to emerge, which needs an army of planners and expediters to try to manage. If you've ever been on the receiving end of this as a planner, customer or supplier, you know exactly what I'm talking about.

So what is the fundamental problem here? Is having and using a forecast really that bad? After all, there has to be some kind of plan and it has to be based on something. No, the problem isn't with the forecast, or indeed the plan. The problem is blindly following the plan and treating planning and execution as a continuous process. Lean takes a different view of planning and while it accepts that a plan is essential and needs to be based on some kind of forecast, it takes into account a well-known and very astute comment made by a military general a while back: "No plan survives the first contact with the enemy." What this tells us is that while a plan is good and makes sure we are prepared as best we can, we must ensure that what we actually do is driven by what is happening rather than what we thought would happen. In other words, planning and execution are two very different and very separate things, each with their own objectives and outcomes. Once you make this separation, things become a lot clearer and cleaner. Let's replay the above taking this approach and see what happens:

* The forecast is used in much the same way as mentioned above, to get some idea of a forward view on what is required. No real change here, it's still a guess, but for what it's going to be used for, that's OK.
* The aggregate forecast is run against the bill of materials to get a view on what is needed to be made or bought to get the finished goods where they are needed, when they are needed. Again, not much is different, "So what's the big deal here?" you might be asking.

But this is the point where the difference starts to happen. The above is used for planning, understanding where and how much inventory needs to be held, understanding what capacity needs to be in place now and in the future, and giving a heads-up to suppliers on what might be coming their way in terms of orders in the future so they can get ready.

From this view of the world, inventory buffers are positioned at strategic points in the supply chain. The amount of buffer needed at each point is calculated so that when real requirements start to arrive there are finished or part-finished products, materials and capacity in place to satisfy those orders within the timeframe that the customer wants them. These buffers are sized to take account of unknowns, demand variability and lead times that are normally experienced.

None of this information is used to actually place any orders, just to get ready for when orders start to arrive. At this point, planning is done because planning is about getting everything prepared to act when action is needed.

Now, let's move on to the execution part, the "doing".

At this point, Lean principle number one kicks in. To save you having to look back to Chapter 2, this principle is: "Be customer demand driven – don't do anything until there is demand from the customer to do it."

This is the point where a Lean, demand-driven supply chain really starts to depart from a forecast–push supply chain. Instead of driving orders from the expected demand, we wait until something is actually sold, or moved to satisfy a sale. This creates a "hole" in one of the buffers and sends a signal to fill it with a new one. This in turn will create another hole or holes somewhere else, which will signal those to be replaced until the cascade of holes ends up with the suppliers to do their bit. In this way, everything that is produced or bought is in response to the customer taking something, so there is no guesswork involved at all here. Also, as everything is needed by a customer or to ensure a customer can be supplied, there are no constantly changing needs.

There are other, quite pleasant knock-on effects of all this too. Now, as you are only making stuff that is needed, you're not wasting precious capacity on making stuff that you don't need. Also, as there is less chopping and changing, there tend to be fewer changeovers needed, releasing even more capacity. This can be used to make more stuff to sell with the same capacity or reduce batch sizes to make the supply more responsive.

All very good indeed! And all very simple too.

One thing to remember about all this though is that the world does not stand still; you can't just set it and forget it. You need to keep refreshing the buffers in terms of where you put them and sizing on a regular basis: at least monthly and possibly even more frequently if you're in a particularly volatile market. Forget to do this at your peril!

> To stock or not to stock, that is the question.

… And a good question it is too. All the above assumes that you are holding stock to satisfy customer needs. This isn't necessarily the case; sometimes you can just wait until you receive an order from the customer and then start working on buying things, putting them together and delivering your product to the customer – make to order. This is the best place for any business to be; life is very simple and you're guaranteed to be making the right stuff if you can get here. However, in order to do this, you need to be able to get all the materials, make the product and get it out to the customer by the time the customer expects to receive the product. If you can do this, then this is the way to go. If not, then you have to have some inventory somewhere. Understanding this relationship between customer expectations and your response time is key to understanding where you need position buffers. As you get better and faster at converting materials to get your products in your customers' hands, the further back in the supply chain you can put the buffer, and the less risk there is of making the wrong stuff. There are a few cases where making the customer wait for your products is good, but we're not all building supercars or making custom jewellery for Hollywood stars.

That takes care of sending requirements to production, but unless you have very flexible equipment or unlimited capacity, just sending a list of what needs to be done isn't quite the end of the matter. The production facility needs to figure out how they are going to fulfil these requirements. In most cases there is an optimal sequence to make all the products needed, to minimise changeovers and cleaning. The people on the line know best here and you need to make sure that there is enough time from when requirements are sent and when the products are needed to allow this sequencing to happen, and that the right people are making the decisions. As an example, let's go back to the paint-mixing scenario we mentioned earlier. You have six colours: black, white, pale green, yellow, brown and dark blue. Would you really want to mix them in the following order: white, black, yellow, dark blue, pale green, brown? Of course not, just think of how long it would take to get the dark colours out of the system to make the light ones. No, you would probably want to do: white, yellow, pale green, dark blue, brown then black. Whatever you do, you'll always have one nasty change to do (black back to white in this case), but if you can keep it to one, so much the better.

There's a section later in Chapter 11 on a good method for managing sequencing and level loading production called "Rhythm" which you might be interested in if this is a big issue for you.

OK that's about it for a whistle-stop tour of Lean planning and execution – very brief, but it should give you some idea of how it all works. But there's a lot more to an enterprise than this, all of which needs to get a dose of Lean to become a Lean Enterprise, at least from a supply chain perspective. Let's look at a few of these other areas and see how they fit.

Priorities and decisions

Otherwise known as sales and operations planning or S&OP. Everyone says they're doing this, but few really are. Very often, there is Sales Planning and Operations Planning, but not the two together. Anyway, this is another debate entirely so to avoid getting totally bogged down on this one, let's just assume that this is happening.

In reality, S&OP is really just the decision-making part of the planning that was described above. People from Sales and people from Operations (no surprises there!) get together roughly once a month to talk about what has happened, what's happening now and what is likely to happen in the future. The outcome of all this is a list of actions, and priorities on what can be done and what can't in order to supply the markets. What tends to happen though, is a lot of discussion on why it all went wrong last month, whether the new forecast is any good and how much time Supply needs to know in advance before they can commit to anything. More often than not, these discussions happen on a very detailed level and the bigger picture tends to get lost.

So how can Lean help here? If you remember from above, the key thing is placement and sizing of buffers and the overall capacity against demand balance, not how accurate is a detailed master plan is. Therefore, the whole discussion changes as different questions are asked.

In terms of the here and now:

1. Has anything changed in our business, which means that we need to move a buffer to a different place? – In most cases, this will be "No", but if it has, it's not too difficult to see where.
2. Have there been any major changes in buffer sizes? – As these are dynamic and regularly updated this is easily tracked; again, this should be obvious.

If the answers to either or both questions above are "Yes", then the discussion starts around making sure that there is clarity on why this has happened. Is it a trend, or driven by a one-off event? What is the impact on the ability to supply? Etc., etc.

This is really all the post-mortem on current affairs that needs to happen apart from a quick look at the metrics to make sure service, quality and cost are tracking as they should. However, the answers to these questions feed into the discussion on the future view of the world, as they provide a window and potential early warning of things to come... maybe.

The next bunch of questions starts to look a bit into the future and ends up being quite strategic:

1. What's going on in the markets that we all need to know about and need to get prepared for? – This is the sales and marketing guy's opportunity to let people know how sales are trending, any major promotions or tenders out there, and anything else that could have a significant impact on demand. The difference here is that this is not a short interval stockkeeping unit (SKU) by SKU-detailed forecast, but a much more top-level aggregate view by product family, much easier to pull together and much more likely to be reasonably accurate!
2. What's going on in supply that could impact the ability to deliver – plant shutdowns, supplier problems, quality or process issues? These are all things that might impact the speed at which things move, or even the capacity to deliver at all.

From these two questions, we can build a future picture of what the demand and capacity balance will look like going forward. From this the critical final question can be asked:

3. Are we going to have a capacity problem?

If the answer is "No", then the new demand, buffer placement and sizes are signed off and used going forward, and everyone can go and get a coffee. If the answer is "Yes", however, then there's a bit more work to do. Depending on the timing and scale of the problem, the actions needed will vary from as simple as authorising some budget for a bit of overtime, to a full-blown executive meeting to make some hard decisions about priorities and/or investments. There will need to be some rules about who can decide what, to ensure that decisions are made, and that they are made at the right level.

What's happened here is that our Lean planning process has provided some clear and simple data which point to the health of the supply chain as a whole. If the numbers don't stack up, then decisions need to be made. The need to make these decisions is no different, but the way to get there is much clearer and avoids a lot of the noise which traditionally gets in the way of seeing the true picture.

Supplier relationships

I'll bet every customer has said, "Life would be simpler if it weren't for the suppliers", and I'll place an equal bet that every supplier has said, "Life would be simpler if it weren't for the customers". Neither can function without the other and if we are talking about an "enterprise", then suppliers are part of that. So why does there seem to be such a problem and does it really have to be this way? The issue is that each tends to see things only from their perspective and in isolation rather than parts of the same whole which need to work together. In our Lean Enterprise world, things need to be a bit different.

As we discussed in a previous chapter, in a Lean world, flow is better and faster. This being the case, there just isn't the time for protracted debate or misunderstandings with suppliers. Indeed, we must embrace our suppliers, bring them along on the journey and help them to be successful, as we can't be successful without them. All very fancy nice fluffy words, but what does this really mean? Let's have a go at explaining a few of the important parts.

What can we now provide?

As explained above, the traditional way of dealing with suppliers was to run MRP, which spat out a load of orders and planned orders, and as lead time approached, release the orders and send to the supplier. This gave them a list of needs with quantities and due dates. From that point on, they were on their own. However, as we also mentioned above, all this was based on a guess, which was constantly being updated. All these updates compounded each other as they were blown through the BoM until the poor supplier at the end of the line was being jerked around constantly. Planners and purchasing people on the phone every day:

"I know we said we needed it in two weeks, but can we have it now?"
"Can we cancel that order please? Oh, the truck's already left?"
"We now need twice as many and by next week. Is that a problem?"
" Yes, I know I'm asking you to undo what I asked you to do yesterday, but ... "

You get the picture. Add to this that most suppliers are measured by their "on time – in full" performance, irrespective of all the changes. So, it's the end of the year and the contract is up for review and the negotiations start with the purchasing guy looking over the supplier's performance numbers. Hmmm, given all the above, just how well do you think that discussion's going to go? The defences go up on both sides and then let battle commence!

Obviously this is no way to do things, but it's surprising how often this happens, particularly when Purchasing is measured on reducing unit price so will use any lever possible to squeeze another drop out of the supplier. Now, how does this play out in the Lean world described above? Let's replay.

If we've done the design right, we have strategic buffers in place which are controlling the flow and decoupling the supply from the chaos. Orders are released to replenish what has been used rather than responding to a guess, the forecast. Since materials have been used up, it makes sense that they should be replaced. Therefore, when an order is placed with a supplier to replenish, there is much less chance that it will be changed or cancelled unless things really go off the rails. OK, there will be the need to hurry a few up or make a few slight changes as unexpected things can still happen, but this will be the exception rather than the rule and when this does happen, the supplier will be in a very different frame of mind when the phone rings. If 90% of the time you place an order and, as long as he delivers on time, he doesn't hear any more about it, then he's much more likely to listen and do something if you call and ask for a favour. So the flow of orders to the supplier is more consistent and not changing, which in turn means that the supplier stands a much better chance of meeting the requirements. Things are better already, material shortages start to decline. Great! We're done. That was easy! Well, not actually – there is a lot more we can do to make things even better.

Getting the best deal

Many purchasing decisions are made on the basis of minimising unit costs, and as anyone knows, the more you buy the bigger discount you get, right? Absolutely right. However, all our Lean thinking to date says that to maintain flow, you need a little, often. This is one of the barriers frequently thrown up against Lean: "If we order in the quantities you say, we'll lose our volume discounts". However, who says that you actually have to take delivery and pay for everything you order all at once? In fact, all those suppliers who are offering volume discounts are trying to do is secure a forward order book. So, if you go to your suppliers and commit to, say, a year's worth of supplies, delivered and paid for on an "as needed" basis, the chances are that you'll still get most, if not all, of your volume discount. In fact, as long as the supplier knows that you will be true to your word, it's better for him if you take delivery in smaller batches as you won't be tying up his capacity for long stretches, which makes it difficult for him to satisfy his other customers' needs. But what does "as needed" mean? The supplier is going to want at least some idea of what you want, when. This is where the forecast still has a role in Lean. Although it's really a guess, your sales forecast translated into supplier requirements should be accurate enough to give the supplier something on which to allocate capacity and work with their own suppliers. Better still, why not give the supplier visibility of your material inventory and let him decide what needs to be delivered? This is called "vendor-managed inventory" (VMI). The only real success criterion here is that you don't run out of stock when you need it. The supplier now has full control and can manage their service to you and other customers much better. This is a real win–win and will usually secure a better unit price than the old "big order".

Support functions

We're still not done. Yes, we've covered the supply chain from end to end, but there's more. What about all those other functions: finance, engineering, HR, and so forth? How is their role different in a Lean world? While it might not seem like it at first glance, the success of long-term Lean is as much in the hands of these functions as the more obvious manufacturing, planning and purchasing people. Let's take a quick look at each and see how this is so.

Finance

This is the big one. The behaviour of the Finance leadership and how they react can mean the difference between a roaring success or a quick kill to any Lean ambitions you might have. It's true to say that in today's world, Finance is king, they control the destiny of businesses and countries throughout the world. If the numbers don't stack up in the way Finance want them to, then it's game over. Let's take a look at an example to see what I mean.

You've worked hard to stimulate flow in your business and the working capital has been flying out of the door and into the customers' hands. But hold on: in financial terms, inventory is an asset, so all your hard work is burning off the asset value of the company. Oops!

Also, as you're burning off all that excess inventory, you have to throttle back on production so that you're not building it back as fast as you're moving it. This means that the overheads are being spread over a lower output, overhead recovery takes a hit, and at standard cost, your nice, slick, efficient plant is now showing as operating at a loss. Oops again.

You've worked hard to sell the idea of smaller batches and only producing what has been sold, which means that the hard stuff to make is now getting its fair share of production time – great! However, production efficiency is usually measured in terms of unit conversion cost. As a consequence of stopping all the easy, long-run, cherry-picking in production, the overall cost divided by volume equation has now moved in entirely the wrong direction. Thrice oops!

What's happening here is that the basic rules of cost accounting are working against us. This says that all costs, variable and fixed, need to be apportioned to the product, and product profitability is measured at a unit level as selling price minus total cost. What's being missed here is that, in reality, only variable cost should be taken into account, as the fixed portion is just that – fixed. Also, costs should be applied to sales, not production, because sales provides the top line of the profit equation. Finance needs to get aligned with the game and make some critical changes in the way the number crunchers look at the business, otherwise all your hard work will be trampled over by the Finance guys in very short order. It's not all doom and gloom, however. When you look at things from the enterprise perspective and start talking in terms the CFO understands, that is "return on investment", the picture is very different. The excess working capital now turns into revenue, adding to the top line. As production throttles back, material costs reduce while overhead remains the same or goes down slightly and, therefore, overall profitability goes up! Bingo! All of this says that while the macroeconomics work out using conventional thinking, how this gets translated into the operating cost accounting and management needs to be seriously looked at. We'll cover this a bit more in the chapter on metrics later.

Engineering

All the talk so far about reliability and flexibility is all very well, but you've got to have the equipment to run that way. Again, our new way of thinking goes against some of the accepted terms of reference for your typical engineering department. Browse the journals and the glossy equipment magazines and you'll find the latest whiz-bang machines, boasting ever-faster and more automated production. The engineers among us – remember I'm an engineer so I can say this – get all worked up and drooling over how impressive that will look in our factories. This lust for ever-faster and more efficient equipment is fuelled by the cost accountants mentioned above, as they see the theoretical cost per unit going down.

But thinking about what we have been saying so far, does the all-singing, all-dancing super-machine really make sense? In my experience, high speed and high automation go hand in hand with hours of changeover time and run times (aka batch sizes), measured in days not minutes or, at most, hours. When we need to be cycling through lots of products quickly to ensure rapid replenishment or short customer order lead times, this doesn't really work, does it? When you take the bigger picture into account, the case is clearly there to sacrifice some of the out-and-out speed for flexibility.

Because of the above, Engineering need to look at things from a slightly different angle than they normally would if they are going to be building and buying the right kit for the new Lean world. While this sounds quite obvious, it can be a very hard sell and many will believe that they are taking a step backwards rather than forwards: lower speed, less complexity, less automation. Traditionally, not something that would be described as music to your average engineer's ears. This is not black and white, however. If you have a few products where the volumes are very high and you can dedicate a high-speed line to the job then go ahead, buy the shiny new machine, but please make sure that you really, really do need it first.

HR

As I'm sure you've already worked out by now, the way people are organised, measured and rewarded is absolutely vital to success. This means that a lot of the conventional rules of HR will need to bend as well. I could go on at length here about this, but I won't. That's because there is a whole chapter or two devoted to the people side of things. Suffice to say here that it's all about every part of the business working together.

In conclusion

As should be obvious by now, when all these things come together, they create a very powerful force. As each part of a business gets itself aligned and starts working towards a common goal, that is "customer delight", they start to reinforce each other rather than work against each other. Many of the common problems and bun fights we see begin to disappear and people start focusing on the external issues rather than the internal turf wars and local efficiencies. When you start thinking this way, one and one really do equal three (or more!). This is what Lean Enterprise is all about and when compared to Lean Manufacturing, the potential is huge. Indeed, I would go so far as to say that Lean Manufacturing can never be a game-changing and sustainable solution as there is still too much of the old world in place to trip things up and squash the right thinking everywhere else in the business.

But this doesn't happen by accident or even by desire: there have to be a few other things in place to force the issue somewhat. If the organisation, leadership and the measures are pulling the hearts and minds in the wrong direction, and the people just don't "get it", there will be a very steep uphill battle to really make a difference. Even if you do change things, there will be a very good chance that the old saying "fixed today, broken again tomorrow" will come into play. We will explore what can be done in some of these areas in the next few chapters.

5

ORGANISING FOR LEAN

We spoke earlier of the need to organise around your desired outcomes and the problems associated with this. In this chapter we will explore this a bit more and propose a model which can overcome some of the issues. This is not the only possible model, and you need to figure out for yourself what the right solution is for your business and your culture. There is no real right or wrong here (except that a traditional, purely functional organisation is probably wrong!).

Turning tradition upside down

When people first see this model (see Figure 3), they tend to fall into the all-too-familiar hierarchical mindset and see the layers as seniority in a conventional organisational structure. Let me say right off the bat, *there is no hierarchy implied in this model*, in fact, quite the reverse. The layers refer to roles, not rank. And all are dedicated to supporting the process execution team either directly or indirectly as they are the ones who are creating the value for the customer, for which the customer is prepared to pay, and which in turn pays for everyone's salary in the end.

What this is trying to say is that the people who create the value should be the centre of the universe for a business and the traditional

Process Execution Team
People engaged in the actual value added work. Pays
the salaries of all the rest

PET Leader (Production or non-production)
Dedicated to supporting the PET. Providing direction
and resolving issues which impact the smooth running
of the process. "Inward looking"

Integration Leader
Accountable for creating the working environment for
the PET and resolving cross-PET issues. "Sideways
looking"

Business Area Strategy Leaders
Planning & medium term strategy development for issues
which will require a shift in direction. "Outward looking"

Company Strategy Leaders
Developing long term business strategy and responses to
total business issues

Figure 3   Layer Organisation Model

boss–subordinate hierarchy should take a back seat. Let's take a
look at the roles in a bit more detail.

We've already talked about the process execution team in
Chapter 2, so no need to expand further on this here. But one role on
the team that is key is that of the team leader. Again, I'd like to stress
that this is not the "boss" as such, although it is where ultimately
the accountability for delivery rests. The PET Leader is fulfilling a
role, just like any other person on the team, no more or less important. Their job is to clear the way for the rest of the team to perform.
The best analogy I can give is a snow plough driver. When it snows,
people can't use the roads and things get snarled up. The job of the
snow plough driver is to clear away the snow so that you can get
on with where you are going. He or she does not come and drive
your car for you, or tell you how to drive it; it's assumed that since
you have a licence you know how to do that. The PET Leader acts
in the same way; the assumption is that the other team members
are capable in what they know to fulfil their role without a lot of
supervision from the Leader. The PET Leader is ruthlessly loyal to
the team and their customers. They have no other requirements but
to get the best possible outcome from the part of the business they
are responsible for delivering.

That's all very well but there will be more than one PET in a business. With all these self-centred people laser-focused on their own part of the business, when resources need to be shared or support is needed by more than one PET at a time, it's going to be war out there. But this is where the next layer comes in. The integration layer. What this person in this layer does is act as the unbiased referee between the PETs. Looking at the bigger picture and determining priorities when conflicts occur, this person does not start getting involved in what is going on inside the PETs, but just monitors performance results and calls the priorities when things get heated. In reality, most PET Leaders are sensible adults, so usually sort out their differences between themselves.

Up to this point, all these layers have been focused on today's customer service and performance, not what might happen in the future. The future is taken care of by the outer two layers, which are more strategic in nature and in many businesses can be collapsed into one. People operating here are looking ahead at what's coming up in the future and getting the business prepared for it. Apart from high-level performance and capabilities, these people are not really concerned about the here and now; they're looking over the hedge to see what's coming over the horizon to hit the business.

So there it is, a new model for organisations based around customer value delivery, both current and future. This works really well as long as the people in those layers understand what their role is and stick to it. Sounds simple, but without some real changes in how people get rewarded and promoted, it indeed is not easy and is almost doomed to failure. Also, it's very hard to stop the people in layers 3 to 5 "meddling" in the process execution as the temptation and history is always there. I remember a conversation I had a while ago with an executive at one of the places I worked:

Exec "Are you telling me I can't go into a site and tell the people there how to do it anymore?"

Me "No, it's not your job."

Exec "Why not, someone's got to make sure things are being done right."

Me "With the right direction, they are capable of managing quite well without you looking over their shoulders."

Exec "Oh, that's a shame, I like doing that and watching them run around." "What happens if they aren't doing it right?"

Me "That means either they're not the right people or don't have the skills or, most likely, they're fine and it's just your opinion. You need to fix one of these problems, not do the job for them. Because while you're doing someone else's job, you're not doing your own and that's how we end up unprepared for something big happening in the world and end up in a panic!"

Exec "That's a bit harsh, I didn't get where I am today by ... "

OK, you get the idea. Eventually he got the message, but it was a hard sell and I nearly lost my job in the process.

As mentioned before, this is not a hierarchical or structural model and it takes a great deal of thought to blend with the company organisational model. Let's take a quick look at how this might work.

Let's get the easy one out of the way first, the process execution team. This is structured exactly as it says on the tin: there is a leader and multifunctional team working in the same organisational unit. However, there remains a dotted line relationship to the functional leadership that takes care of innovation, setting the standards and ensuring that the skills remain recent and relevant.

While we're on the subject, contrary to some views, there is definitely a need to retain the functional organisational entities, with a leadership structure to take care of the above and to look at the more technical, tactical and strategic issues related to supporting the business. In terms of role structure within these functional groups, the same principles as described above will work but they are focused on support activities and strategies, not getting stuff out the door.

However, what we find is that these functional groups tend to be smaller and flatter, as much of the day-to-day work is done by their representatives in the process execution teams. I have seen some organisations try to take the purely process-centric view and have the whole organisation aligned to process execution teams. While good in theory, it really doesn't work out in practice, as standards tend to erode and there is no mechanism to ensure that skills are not lost as people move in and out of the company.

The final part of the more simple layers to solve is the senior leadership, the C-somethings and the VPs; this is usually the top layer in an organisation and as long as it is only one layer, it will probably stay pretty much untouched. In fact, many of these positions are dictated by company law and shareholders, so there usually isn't much room for whole-scale structural change. Also, this fits with the role layers we talked about above, as this group forms the basis of the fourth and fifth layers.

So, on to the more tricky part of the organisation, what sits between the process execution team and the top dogs? There is no single right answer here. What ends up being right for your business will depend on a lot of things including the size of your organisation, the diversity of the work you do, whether you're global, regional or locally structured as a business, the culture of the business and the geographical area, to name but a few. However, it's not all just a matter of "do what you want", there are a couple of guiding principles that you should take into account before deciding on the right way for you, and these are outlined below.

Try to keep the number of hierarchical layers to a minimum. As a general best practice, there should be no more than four management layers to the top. To put this in the context of a typical structure and title, we have: (1) the CEO; (2) all the functional heads; (3) departmental managers; (4) line supervisors; and then all the people actually doing the work. This is a huge change for a lot of companies and few large organisations actually get here, but if you can get to five, and you are a fairly large organisation working internationally, then you're not doing badly.

The second rule of thumb is that a leader can only effectively lead between 10 and 15 people directly. The caveat to this is where there is a high level of manual work involved, requiring large numbers of people doing relatively simple and repetitive work. If you apply this rule and the one above, the structure starts to define itself. If you run the numbers, you can see that even in the worst case this approach will accommodate pretty large organisations before it breaks down, around 11,000 people. Obviously, designing an organisation is a lot more complex than just using a formula like the one above, but it will give you a blueprint on which to overlay your needs. If nothing else, it will throw up a challenge that will force you to justify the differences – if the reasons stack up, then there isn't a problem.

Getting ahead in a PCO

All of the above is well and good, but humans are, by nature, aggressive, ambitious and want to get ahead of each other. In other words, most people want to be successful and to be recognised for it. Herein lies a problem.

Lean, process-centric organisations tend to be a lot flatter than traditional ones. As a result, there are far fewer chiefs and a lot more Indians. This means that opportunities for progression in the conventional way of "getting on" by promotion through the ranks to positions of seniority are now few and far between; accelerated career paths for your most talented are just not there in the traditional sense. Seeing no way to get to the next level, your best people will, quite naturally, look elsewhere for the next step up and leave. Not good! So, do we put back all the hierarchy and empires we have just demolished just to keep the chosen few happy? Probably not a good idea either. No, what needs to happen is the creation of new, non-hierarchical career paths, ones in which the contribution to the business through innovation, skills and potential value are rewarded as much as leadership. In this way, parallel routes to the top exist, helping you retain your best people. Let's look at this a little closer, as the full implications of this are not obvious. In a Lean environment, agility and flexibility are very important, so the ability for a person to switch from one role to another is very valuable. Therefore, you need to reward this flexibility, which means that a person is paid not just for the job they are doing today, but for all those they are capable of doing if needed. This really challenges the conventional pay linked to job approach. A nice by-product of this approach is an elimination of the well-known "promoted to his/her level of incompetence" syndrome, where someone who can "do" well, ends up managing others who "do" even if they are bad at managing. With the above approach, there are technical routes as well as leadership routes up the ladder.

To take this a step further, the need for flexibility and team working needs to be reflected in job titles too. An extreme I encountered at a company which had taken PCO very seriously only had three job titles: Process Execution Team Member; Integration Team Member; Strategy Team Member. These aligned to the 5-layer model as outlined above and whoever you spoke to at whatever position in the organisation, they introduced themselves in one of these three roles. Digging deeper, there were no job descriptions either, but role descriptions – a subtle difference with profound implications. This meant that a role could be filled by more than one person or one person could fill more than one role. In addition, one person could be capable of fulfilling more than one role and was paid more as a result, even though at the time, they were doing the same job as the person next to them who was more limited in what they could do. At first this seems a little unfair, but in reality, it encouraged people to get trained in other roles, adding to the flexibility of the whole business, which is a good thing. One word of caution here, though, If allowed to go on unchecked, you could end up with everybody spending a greater proportion of their time training to get better pay than doing customer value-adding work, so there need to be some rules around how this is done. As an example: one of the roles of the PET Leader is to understand the required skills profile of the team as a whole to provide the necessary flexibility and redundancy to cater for whatever situation is likely to arise. By comparing this to the actual, a plan is created to train up the required number of people to fill the gaps and rewards are based upon how the individuals in the team acquire the skills demanded by the plan. So it's not a free-for-all.

Performance rewards are another tricky area. In most organisations you have individual rewards based on individual performance against an individual's targets. As we have said earlier, we are more interested in the process outcomes as this is what the customer sees. So, rewarding an outstanding individual performance with a big bonus when the process outcome went South doesn't really work, does it? Conversely, rewarding everyone in a team the same when one guy busted a gut while the others sat at their desks with their feet up chatting doesn't seem fair either. The solution is to have the right balance of team and individual measures. The team as a whole is measured on the overall process performance and this sets the total "pot" available to be distributed within the team. The better the overall outcome, the bigger the pot. How the pot is then distributed amongst the team is based on the contribution the individuals make to the performance of the team. For example, let's say the outcome measures are on target; this would give the team a rating of "fully met" so there would be a pot available to be distributed across the team in line with this. However, not all members of the team performed equally, so it would not be fair to the good performers to distribute the pot equally, neither would it be sending the right message to the slacker to get his act together. But how do we rate the team members? Remember it's not just about individuals meeting their personal objectives; it's how they support the team as well. Let's take an example. Two team members, A and B, both meet all their targets, but A came to the aid of team member C who was having trouble and helped out to ensure that C and the overall team performed well. B, however, did what was expected of him then went home without considering that C was in trouble and needed help. In this case, the PET Leader would give A a larger share of the pot than B; even C would get more, as he had recognised that he was in trouble and asked for help to ensure the team did not suffer. In a PCO it's as much about behaviours as it is about applying skills and knowledge.

The football team

To give an example of what I mean here, let's take a situation most people will be very familiar with. It involves football, or soccer for those of you from the western side of the Atlantic. The points and outcomes I'm going to make could apply to just about any team sport, but I think the results are more pronounced in football/soccer, purely as a result of the nature of the game.

As everyone knows, the objective of the game is to put the ball into the net of your opposition more times than they do it to you. If you manage this, you win, if not, you lose. The objective of a football club is to win more games than the rest and finish the season at the top of the league table. If you manage this, you get a nice bit of silverware to parade around the town and to put in a cabinet. You also get the undying love of the fans (well, at least for the next few weeks until you lose again!). Oh yes, I nearly forgot, the club gets a shedload of money from the relevant Football Association and TV stations to spend on a new stadium, better players and to line the owners' pockets.

Now one might think that if you can go out and scour the world, buy all the best players, offer them huge salaries and goal-scoring bonuses, you would be on to a winner. This is exactly what one team did a few years ago and it was a disaster. They actually ended up lower in the league during the first season since the big spend than they did the year before. Not only that, there was a lot of unrest in the dressing room, resulting in three of the recently bought players asking for a transfer, and the manager was shown the door. So what went wrong?

What happened was that the owners and the manager forgot that a football team is more than the sum of its parts, and that it's not just about individual skill – it's about how those skills augment each other. Let's look a little deeper. By having all those great players and offering goal bonuses, all of them were trying to outshine each other, trying to make sure they were selected for the starting team for the next match and not left sitting on the bench. But as anyone knows, if you put enough bodies in the way, even the most skilful player in the world will end up losing the ball if they try to go it alone. The other thing here is that a good team needs a balanced range of skills and every player needs to understand their own strengths and weaknesses and those of all the other players in the team. By knowing this and having a strategy for the game, each player uses their strengths to cover for the weaknesses of the others. If you can achieve this, then the team acts like a single player with extraordinary skills able to be in ten places at once. This understanding takes time to develop over months, if not years, of training on the practice ground and playing together in matches. So that takes care of having the right collective skills, but what about the behaviour? If you add to the mix an incentive just to win as a team, where all the team shares a win bonus whether they are the goal scorer or sitting on the bench, this changes the entire mindset. Now, rather than a player making a fuss about being brought off at half time, they might even suggest it themselves if it looks like the initial strategy isn't working and a different skill mix is needed to win the game. When all this comes together, it's amazing what can be achieved with even mediocre players. A team working together with a common goal will beat the team of individual prima donnas nearly every time.

I'm sure that this is all very obvious to most of you, but why then do we see examples of the "prima donna" team in businesses every day, where the objective seems to be "make me look good in front of the boss"? The solution seems obvious as well, but it's not always that simple.

Theory vs. reality

As mentioned earlier, all this is very nice in theory but extremely difficult to do in practice. It means turning your whole organisation on its head and undoing a lifetime of conventional behavioural conditioning in the process. For most companies, especially the bigger ones, applying the above to the fullest extent is just not possible. However, it's not mandatory to employ all of the above, it's as much about the mindset as it is the physical change. If you can think of a few ways to incorporate some of the thinking into your organisation, especially the process execution team part, then your operation will benefit from faster decision making and a better working environment for your people. Better working environment? Really? Where's the evidence? Over the years I've been involved in a number of organisation changes along the lines described above and have made a point of going back later and asking people at all levels who have made the change to a PET structure if they would return to the old way of working. In every case the answer was an emphatic "no". In one case I nearly got lynched by the team for even suggesting the idea! Usually this reaction is then qualified with an explanation that it means doing things that are not strictly your job, greater commitment and, in some cases, working harder, but when balanced against the greater self-determination, variety of work and freedom to control one's own future, the majority would not go back to the old ways.

The unfortunate but inevitable consequences

My conscience won't let me leave this section without acknowledging the painful part of all this. People are people and we are all different. Those differences are reflected in our behaviours, ambitions and what we value. With a few exceptions, these differences don't make one group good and the others bad, they're just different, and it's this diversity which makes the world an interesting place. So, given this is a fact of nature, the PCO concept and all it implies will not suit everyone. There will be leaders who will not want to give up what they have and learn a different way of leading. There will be people who are quite happy turning up for work every day and being told by their manager what to do. Let me make it quite clear, there is nothing wrong with this. However, these people will have a very hard time coming to terms with the new environment and will be unhappy. This unhappiness is contagious and will rub off on others. In my experience this has been the case in every business that has made this transition. So how do you deal with this?

Firstly, be sure that you have made the right diagnosis. The early symptoms of not understanding and not accepting are the same; the first group can turn into advocates and some of the best performers in a PCO environment with some TLC and coaching. Try every possible way to bring them round, but accept that there will be a few who just won't get there.

Once at this point there is nothing left to do but to do the humane thing and let them go. It's not fair to the individual or to the rest of the team to force them to stay in a world where they are uncomfortable. This is not firing them, it is recognising that there has been a divergence of ideas and no one is at fault but there must be a parting of the ways. Your responsibility here is clear, you have to make the transition out of the company and into other work as easy and painless as possible for the individuals concerned. This means generous severance terms, assistance with job searches, good references and so forth. In the long term, it's in the best interests of everyone and in most cases I've come across, the individuals concerned end up in a better place and happier as a result. This issue is not confined to the lower ranks of an organisation. It happens at 'C' level, coal-face level and everywhere in between. On a more positive note, only a very small percentage of your organisation will be impacted to this extent, so it's not big, just important.

In conclusion

What we have covered in this chapter are some thoughts on how to organise to take best advantage of Lean concepts and increase the velocity in your operation. While some level of reorganisation and role change is inevitable, you shouldn't leave this chapter thinking that you need to change the world. The ideas outlined above are just examples of what could be done, not what must be done. At the end of the day, if the people in your organisation have a Lean mindset and are allowed to work in a Lean way, then it does not really matter how you structure the organisation, good things will happen. This mindset is the subject of a later chapter.

6

MEASURING THE RIGHT STUFF AND METRICS

A s promised in Chapter 2 when we introduced the core concepts, we've now returned to the measures. Most people understand the importance of measuring performance; indeed, we are brought up from a very tender age to understand this from winning games and passing school exams, through to your annual performance assessment. We have measures and statistics thrown at us in a constant barrage every day. In most companies I've worked in, the list of "KPIs" can be over a hundred, and that's not going down to the lowest level of operation. The reason I put "KPIs" in quotes is that the "K" means Key, so if one hundred are just the "Key" ones, just imagine how many of the "non-Key" ones there must be. Do we really need so many? Are we sure we are measuring the right things? Well, in my experience, the reason for the former is to try to make sure we do the latter, on the basis that if you measure everything, somewhere in all that you'll be measuring the right things. Before we dive into what the right things are, let's take a quick look at why we need to measure in the first place – what is it we are trying to do?

There are really only two answers to this:

- Firstly, it's to find out if we are performing to some target we set for ourselves or someone else set for us.
- Secondly, it's to try to encourage somebody or a group of people to behave in a particular and/or consistent way.

There is another class of measure, which is not a measure at all really; it's a control. In simple terms, it's a tripwire to make something happen when a certain set of conditions is met; we'll talk about controls later in the chapter, but first let's focus on measures.

As I mentioned before, successful Lean requires that there are simple and clear rules and that there is the discipline to follow them. Therefore, it's this second one which plays the important role in a Lean environment. That's not to downplay the first one too much, though.

These two reasons also give us a clue into the difference between measures and metrics. Many people use the two terms synonymously, but there really is a difference:

- A measure is a thing we put a value to. In other words, what we are measuring and its value, either current or past.
- A metric is comprised of three parts: a measure, as defined above; a target; and a consequence of either achieving or not achieving the target.

There are examples of this one all around us. The following is an example we have all experienced at school.

There is an end of lesson test and the teacher hands out the papers and we all do the test. The next day, I get my mark and it's 67%. This is a measure. I've been given a test to see how well I've been paying attention and I've scored 67%.

Now let's turn the above into a metric: the first part reads the same, the teacher hands out the papers ready for the test. Now, the difference starts. Before we started the lesson, the teacher told us all "There will be a test at the end of the lesson and the acceptable mark for this test, if you have been paying attention to me this afternoon, is 75%. If you don't achieve this, you will come back after school has finished to study your notes and resit the test." Now, this is a metric, because we have a target and a consequence. Also, I just got some detention. Or did I? If I had known at the start that there was a target and a risk of detention, maybe I would have paid a bit more attention during class and got the required 75%, maybe. Now we are starting to see the power of metrics applied to the right measure and the influence on behaviour.

From this we can see that if we want to incentivise the right Lean behaviours, we need to focus on the right measures, provide very clear targets and ensure there are appropriate consequences. Most of the time we hear of consequences, they are usually bad and designed to stop us doing something: "If you don't stop pulling your sister's hair, you'll be sent to your room for the rest of the day"; "If you break the speed limit, you'll get a fine and points on your licence" – we've all heard them many times. They don't have to be all negative, however. In fact, positive consequences for doing the right thing or for high achievement are more motivating than the reverse, so be creative with the positive consequences! Now we've got that straightened out, what should we be focusing on?

What's important?

There were some clues to this in Chapter 2. These were getting answers to the three fundamental questions:

- Are we delivering enough?
- Are we delivering the right things?
- Are we doing this with the minimum of waste?

So, all we need to do is think up some appropriate measures to answer these questions and we'll be all set, as long as we have some targets and consequences associated with them, right? In principle, yes. The first two should be relatively straightforward to get right if we think about it properly; the last one, however, can be an absolute minefield if we're not careful. So, let's leave the difficult one for now and get the two easier ones out of the way.

"Are we delivering enough?" For this we need to (a) look at the demand for all our products and add it all together, this gives us the total amount we need to do; then (b) look at the total output we are producing and compare the two. If (a) is greater than (b) then the answer is "no". If (a) is less than or equal to (b) then the answer to the question is "maybe". What? "Maybe"? How's that? Well, if you remember back in Chapter 2, we talked about overproduction being a waste. There may be a very good and Lean-valid reason why (b) is greater than (a), but we need to check first before we turn the "Maybe" into a "Yes". We can't turn this into a useful metric quite yet, as we need to answer the second question before we do that.

"Are we delivering the right things?" This is a little more tricky, but given we have explained in previous chapters about Lean planning and scheduling, we have ways to do this. If we have set up buffers for finished goods and materials in the way we described earlier and made sure that they reflect the current market situation, then we can see if we are delivering the right stuff quite easily, as the buffers will be moving up and down nicely in the green and yellow segments with the occasional dip into the red. If this is what we see, then the answer to this question will be "yes". If we see lots of dips into the red and going negative, and/or big peaks over the green, then the answer is "no".

If we are running in a demand-driven way and following the rules, then we should have a lot more "yes" answers than "no" answers to these two questions.

Now we have answers to both, we can turn them into metrics. At the highest level, if there are a lot of "no" answers, the consequences are dissatisfied customers, lost sales and, in the extreme, we go out of business. Conversely, if the answers are mostly "yes", then the reverse is true, although we could still go out of business if the answer to the third question is very wrong.

Further into the organisation, the consequences have to be more personal and immediate. For example, someone needs to be made accountable for making sure that the buffers are all being managed properly and that the rules are being adhered to. This is where we see the connections starting to be made between what individuals do and the ultimate impact on the business as a whole.

This all looks quite straightforward, and indeed it is. But we are by no means finished. We have the tricky third question to answer, and this is where it can all get very complicated very quickly, and also go completely off the rails. So, here goes.

"Are we doing this with the minimum of waste?" If you remember, we defined waste earlier; in fact, there were three main categories of it. Hmm... starting to get a bit complicated already. Now, layer on top that we need to be looking across the entire end-to-end supply chain, including all the support areas... things just got a bit more complicated!

To help us out of this potential quagmire, we need to keep calm and focus. Focus on what? Well, focus on the customer: after all, that is what we are all here for, and when I say customer, I mean the end customer, the one that's paying for our stuff, not the guy next up the chain or, even worse, your boss! How does this help?

For a start, if we can set up a suite of measures which look at value from the customer perspective, we might be on to something, Then, if we introduce our dear old friend, flow, and measure how that value is flowing to the customer, we might just have it cracked, as waste in any form destroys either value, flow, or both. Finally, if we cascade those through the organisation to manage the activities of everyone, there will be at least a fighting chance that most people will be working to the same end, that end being the right thing.

So, if we use this as the yardstick to test what we are setting up, we should be able to spot the inconsistencies and conflicts with a bit of investigative work and fix them. Here are a few examples of what I'm talking about.

Output is something we should be interested in, right? Are we applying our assets to do the most useful work? The typical measure used here is output per hour and it is applied to individuals (as in piece work or services), equipment (as Overall Equipment Effectiveness, OEE), departments or indeed whole companies. On the surface this seems OK, but let's look a little deeper given what we have been talking about before. Output is only of value if the customer needs it; otherwise it just sits around and gathers waste until it becomes waste itself. In fact, a lot of what people do is waste anyway, like measuring how many widgets are shipped between one store and another, or how quickly a report is produced. So, while output per employee is fine for finding out how busy people are, all it will do is to make people find something, not necessarily useful, to do in order to keep busy. In addition, by doing these non-value things, we are interrupting the flow of the value-added things we should be doing. Hmm ... not so good now, is it?

However, if you change one small aspect of this – the numerator from units to sales value – it now suddenly works. If the work that people or assets are so busy doing doesn't translate to sales, then it doesn't count. Problem solved! Also, we are now looking end-to-end by linking all the measures to sales, the end game. But how many times do you see macro productivity and bonus payments in the supply measured in sales? Not very often, nine out of ten times it's units. While we're on the subject, let's take a look at OEE, as this is very popular but has a bit of an application problem. OEE, put simply, looks at actual output and compares it to the theoretical maximum possible and expresses this as a percentage. If you have equipment dedicated to specific products and you can sell all you make, then simply measuring OEE in the classical way probably works for 90% of cases. However, most of us don't have these luxuries. Equipment needs to make a range of products, some easier to make than others, and we are often working in a limited or competitive market where we can only sell limited quantities of some things. In these cases the simple approach above starts to break down, as it can drive people to make the fast-running, high-volume products at the expense of the more difficult and low-volume stuff, just to make the numbers look good. Once we make the same change as above and only give output credit if it is to satisfy a customer order or to replenish a buffer, it all starts to work. All very simple, but rarely done. Strategic buffers help with the cascade process too. The time lag between making or doing something and the revenue for it appearing on the sales ledger can be very long; we need something a bit more immediate if we are going to know if our production line, or service processing office, or whatever it is we do is doing OK on a day-to-day local basis, and that leads us right back to units. Having demand-driven buffers solves this, as, by definition, they are only there to ensure good, uninterrupted supply of value to customers. Therefore, we only count what's needed to replenish the next buffer, and then any overproduction just to keep busy won't count. We now have a hard linkage between local activities and delivery of customer value. In the service sector, this isn't so much of a problem, as most activity is linked to a customer order or service request and is effectively made to order. By measuring flow of value, as described above, we are able to see if we are effectively eliminating waste from whatever we do, and if we are getting better at it as time goes on.

"But what about quality?" I hear you ask. Indeed, some form of quality, or fit-for-purpose measures need to be added to the mix. But again, when we look at value, quality is part of it, so only a minor modification is needed here. By adding a second caveat to the output measure, "fit for purpose", we're still OK. What needs to happen now is to define what characteristics constitute fit for purpose and measure those. Our voice of the customer (VOC) and CCRs will help here.

So you can see from all this that it only required a few well-targeted measures at the right places to effectively see if we are succeeding or not. Ultimately, if these are heading in the right direction, it will be reflected in the overall financial results.

Well, that covers the process and product part of measures, but as we've mentioned before, there's more to it than that.

Individual performance vs. team outcomes

This is the final part on types of measures and looks at the impact that measures and metrics have on behaviour, as well as the results.

We touched on an example of this in the chapter on Lean enterprise, where the unit cost and overhead recovery measures were fighting against the need to accelerate flow and meet true demand for the whole product portfolio. We also mentioned this in the chapter on organisation, but at the risk of redundancy, let's look at another one very much linked to the football example in the same chapter and one I experienced an example of personally, which really opened my eyes many years ago. It goes on a bit, but it really was an epiphany.

Way back when, most professional services firms were in offices and regions. There were offices in major cities, with a senior executive running each office. These offices were grouped into regions and countries, with even more senior execs running these; over the top of it all was the MD or senior partner. The primary drivers for executive remuneration were revenue generation and profit contribution from the part of the business for which each executive was responsible. Everything worked reasonably well, revenues steadily rose year on year and because profit was also in the equation, the tendency to discount heavily just to get revenue was kept in check. So what was the problem, you ask? The answer was, nothing really – on the surface. However, when you started to look closer, what was happening was that each office executive was taking care of their own patch and their own people and not looking beyond that. As a result, the size of the jobs taken on was limited to the resources available to the office and people got staffed on a project because they were available in that office, even if there might have been a better qualified person available in another office. There was some cross-working and collaboration, but this was not the norm, and working out the finances got very tricky and usually involved a lot of haggling between the executives to make sure they got the best slice of the pie associated with their office.

About the same time, many of the client companies started to turn into global businesses with operations all over the world and in many locations in the same country. Given this, it doesn't take a rocket scientist to figure out that our office-based reward and management structure was starting to show some flaws. What started to happen was that our firm was picking up a number of relatively small projects from different parts of the same client, which were worked as independent projects by the local offices. What they missed was the monster opportunity to work at solving the client's endemic issues because no one was seeing the bigger picture. Even if they did, the measurement and reward structure encouraged them to maximise the local, even to the detriment of the whole. Why would I, as an executive, ask for help to bid on a bigger project, when this would mean sharing the spoils? It just didn't happen.

The change finally came when a new person took over the top job. Fortunately, he was a little more enlightened and saw the opportunity. He stood up and made a sweeping announcement at his first major company shindig. Let's see if I can remember the exact words: "We are missing the big opportunities with our most important clients because we are working as a collection of small businesses rather than a major player in this industry. We are not leveraging the client or solution knowledge we each have. This has to stop, and it stops right now". A very nice speech indeed, but unlike some before him, he made a couple of sweeping changes at the same time to make it happen.

Firstly, he cut the individual office and county components of the executives' remuneration down to only 25% from 75%. The rest was based on the overall firm performance. This on its own had a dramatic impact on how they behaved towards one another. But he didn't stop there.

Secondly, he set up a small Bid Review Panel, whose job it was to review proposals going to the top 50 strategic clients and look for ways of combining or leveraging the services into other parts of the client or covering a broader scope. If opportunities were found, the relevant partners were put in touch with each other to work on a combined approach.

The results were incredible. Overall firm growth rate more than doubled, the average size of projects undertaken increased by a factor of five and profitability increased by 25% on those projects. After about eighteen months of getting used to the idea of working together, the Bid Review Panel was scrapped as it wasn't really needed any more.

All of this happened because the measures and metrics were realigned to solving the clients' bigger picture issues and encouraging people to collaborate.

The balanced scorecard

I can't leave the measures bit of this chapter without a quick mention of the "balanced scorecard", and believe me, it will be only a quick mention. All a balanced scorecard is trying to do is make a check that in your efforts to do the right thing, you are taking care of the business as a whole, not just part of it. I'm going to focus on what's called the "first generation" balanced scorecard, as I think this was closer to what the real need is. Later, it evolved into a couple of generations that linked everything to strategic goals and ultimately results-based management. While these are not necessarily bad, it starts to layer on the complexity and detract from the primary purpose – in my opinion, that is!

Anyway, the balanced scorecard addresses four aspects of the business which you need to take care of in roughly equal measures:

- Your customers
- Your money
- Your processes and assets
- Your people.

The idea is that if you have about the same number of key measures in each of these areas, then you are taking a balanced view of your business, hence the name. By its nature, the balanced scorecard is going to be populated with outcome measures so is only going to tell you where you've been, not necessarily where you're going.

If you're going to have one of these, please, please make sure that you stick to the vital few in each sector – two or three – and that they are complying with the sentiments made above in terms of understanding the three important things and driving the right behaviours. As an example of what you might want to include in each area, consider the following:

Customer – service level, complaints, speed to market.

Money – revenue, margin, cash to cash cycle time.

Processes and assets – utilisation (be careful, see above!), efficiency (ditto on care!), defect rate, right first time.

People – skills at target, health and safety measure, absenteeism (linked to the second one), turnover rate (linked to job satisfaction).

There are literally hundreds of things you could use and the above is just a teaser that probably won't match your specific needs. It's vital that you think very carefully during the selection process to ensure you are picking measures that are right for you and what you want to achieve.

Controls

If you remember, at the start of this chapter I mentioned that there was another class of measure called controls, so let's look at these now. Controls are not really measures as such, but more a means of monitoring the current status of something. It's much like the fuel gauge or speedometer in your car: they're not necessarily telling you if you are doing well or not, just giving you information on which to make a decision. In this example, a fuel gauge on 1/4 full and a speedometer reading of 65 mph doesn't mean anything unless it's supported by some contextual information. For example, if you were 300 miles away from the nearest refuel and driving through a town with a speed limit of 30 mph, this would indicate that you might have a bit of a problem!

Traditional measures tend to provide more of a rear-view mirror perspective. Because Lean processes require quick decisions to be made at the place of work, this implies that Lean needs a bit more than this, something to enable questions like:

"Are we going to meet today's expectations?"
"Are we behind?"
"Is the next job ready to go?"
"Are all the parameters within limits?"

but more importantly:

"Do I need to do something?"

In order to do this, Lean relies heavily on controls and, in particular, visual controls. These take many forms, but in essence, they provide clear signals to anyone passing by as to the current status of something, or whether attention is needed. With good visual controls, a person who needs to understand whether they need to act should be able to walk out into the area, look around and understand the current situation and where intervention is needed, without asking anyone anything or having to look something up. In a place where there is a lot going on, this means that visual controls need to be clear, simple, available and unambiguous. Again, nice words, but what do they mean? Let's look at a few everyday examples.

One great example of all of these criteria is one that I get reminded of every time I walk through my home village, and that is the church roof fund thermometer. I'm sure you've all seen these a thousand times. A 6-foot-tall representation of a thermometer, with a big target line at the top and a simple scale up the side representing cash. The amount collected to date is represented by a broad red line running up the middle. This is a classic example of a visual control to show current status. You don't even need to read the scale to know where they are against the target and if they are getting closer. One glance from across the street tells you if they need to start ordering the materials or whether it'll be the next century before the roof gets fixed.

Another one is the red light over the checkouts in a supermarket. All a manager or an assistant needs to do is stand where they can see the line of checkouts. If a light comes on, they know exactly where to go. If a lot of lights come on, there's a real problem and whoever it is probably needs to call in the cavalry! This example has a name in the Lean world, it's called an Andon Light and can be seen all over most factories. These typically have three colours: red, amber and green, and denote, respectively "Help!", "Being sorted, but not running" and "OK".

An example of using visual controls to make something, which actually could be quite complicated, clear and simple, is racing car instrumentation. Now, this has all changed as there are LEDs everywhere and telemetry back to the pits, but in the good old days when the driver had to know what was happening to the car and make the decisions, he or she only had a set of very standard-looking instruments to rely on, as you would find in any normal car at the time. Things like oil pressure and temperature, water temperature, and so on, are very important to keep a close watch on as you tear round the circuit. Now, while trying to navigate a series of tight bends at 150 mph, you can't be staring at your instruments and looking at the numbers to see what's what, can you? So here's how they solved it. If you get the chance, have a look into the cockpit of an old racing car, I'll bet you see that all the instruments are at odd angles. The reason for this is that "normal" for everything is straight up. Therefore, a driver only needs to look down for a fraction of a second to see if everything is OK. All the needles pointing up, pedal to the metal. Something not pointing up, time to go to the pits.

What all these things have in common is that they are telling one thing at a time, so there is no confusion over the message or the action needed. The other thing in common is that they are pictorial not textual. You don't have to be able to read or understand a language to get the message. Imagine a traffic light signal where the red light was replaced with "Please do not proceed" and you're from China on a visit!

Telling one thing at a time is quite important, especially if decisions need to be made quite quickly. With the current trend of ever-increasing amounts of available data, it's very easy to get carried away and provide information just because you can, like putting five lines and compound scales on a chart, or filling a car dashboard with 30 different indicators and lights; the former is confusing and takes time to understand what it's telling you, the latter leads to information overload with potentially disastrous results if multiple things happen at the same time.

I could go on for pages with different examples of visual controls, but I suspect by now you've got the message, so I'll stop here. Before wrapping up this chapter, I just want to make a quick comment on reports. Again, with massive amounts of data readily available, reporting capabilities have gone off the scale, and whole industries have built up around it. Here again, the "I can, therefore I want" syndrome has become a real problem. There are a few things you need to remember about reports. Firstly, they are out of date as soon as they leave the printer. Secondly, they are very often produced for very specific purposes, so can be misinterpreted when reviewed out of context. Finally, linked to the second one, reports often continue to be produced and circulated long after the original purpose has expired. Now, this is not to say that reports are always a bad thing; they have their place in the Lean world, but just take care when designing them and always ask, "Is there some other way to communicate this?".

Decision trees

I wasn't quite sure where to put this section, here or in the Tools chapter. It's more about asking the right questions and seeing the wood from the trees. Anyway, I opted to put it here.

This is a very useful tool, which can really help you get your head around a problem or situation. It can be applied very broadly and help with standardisation as well as the more familiar use in giving you the big picture view.

Knowing what to do when something unexpected happens is probably just as important as following the procedures in the status quo. It's these bumps in the road that can set everything off kilter, and by applying knee-jerk reactions instead of pre-thought-through plans, everything can go off the rails. A bit of "If this happens, do that" planning can save a lot of heartache later.

What we are doing here is writing the "play book" for a certain situation based on a set of parameters being either true or false. Virtually every situation in life can be mapped out and analysed through a series of "yes" or "no" responses to questions, and different paths taken dependent on the answers. This is how artificial intelligence (AI) works, and our own brains are really nothing more than billions of switches, which are either off or on depending on the stimuli our senses provide. Now I'm not suggesting anything that complicated, but the same logic can give us some clear guidance to deal with potential future events and solve some quite tricky problems.

We've talked before about how having the right set of metrics and indicators is vital, but seeing them as a set and interpreting them properly is even more important. Doing this right is more of a culture change challenge than anything else, as people typically react to a single input rather than looking at the bigger picture.

Let's look at an everyday example first. Almost everyone will be familiar with the car dashboard. On it are a suite of dials and lights that are telling you what's going on with the car at the time. Let's now look at how we can understand what's going on and what action to take by looking at what's happening to a group of instruments in a particular situation and applying the decision tree approach. Here's the scenario. You've been driving all day, you just filled up the tank with fuel (the right fuel!) about 5 minutes ago. You are driving up a steep hill and the car starts to lose power. What's going on? Well, I'll wager that the first thing that would jump into most people's minds is "I'll bet I've just filled up with bad fuel", followed by a list of choice expletives. However, let's look a little closer at what the instruments on the dashboard can tell us and how this might change our view of what's wrong and the actions we might take.

Temp	Speedo	Tacho	Probable Issue(s)	Recommended Action(s)
Normal	Decreasing	Decreasing	Bad fuel Brakes binding	Turn around and get back to the filling station, syphon off as much as possible and get fresh fuel. Stop, check the brakes and adjust if you have the tools, if not soldier on or call for help.
High	Decreasing	Decreasing	Steep hill overstressing engine Low water level in radiator	Stop, let engine cool a bit then try again. Stop, top up water and carry on.
Zero	Decreasing	Decreasing	No water in radiator, probable big leak or blown hose	Stop, call for help or do a temporary fix if you can to get you home.
Normal	Decreasing	Increasing	Slipping clutch	Depress clutch a few times to see if it's just a bit stiff. Stop and call for help. Carefully try and nurse it home while praying you don't come across another steep hill.

As you can see from all this, while the symptom was the same in all cases, the indicators were telling you very different stories, which required very different actions. You only get this from interpreting all the instruments, not just relying on one. Even so, in some cases there is still a bit of investigation to do to pinpoint the real problem.

This table actually represents a decision tree. By asking a series of questions like "Is the tacho decreasing while the speed is decreasing?" and then, depending on the answer, either jumping straight to a problem and taking action or, additionally asking about the temperature, we can arrive at different end points depending on the answers. If you have a series of different scenarios already thought through and laid out in the "troubleshooting" section of the car handbook, somebody that doesn't necessarily understand how cars work can still do the right thing.

Here's an example we might come across in some of the larger organisations. In a lot of cases, different parts of the organisation are looking at the same measures but have very different metrics in terms of targets and consequences. For example: Sales might focus on service, sales value and forecast error and are rewarded for driving each in the right direction. They might have a passing interest in finished goods inventory as long as service is guaranteed. Supply, on the other hand, might focus on cost, work in process and finished goods inventory, as these drive the cost of goods. They also are interested in how they supply Sales in terms of service to the distribution centres, but not necessarily right through to the end customer. Again, Supply is measured on these and usually there is a lot of pressure to reduce costs here. If you blank out each other's focus area of the view of the same story, different conclusions about the state of the supply chain can be drawn. Let's look at the Supply view of the world first.

Finished Inventory	Work in Process	Cost	What's Happening and Actions
Up	Level	Level	No clue, perhaps Sales are selling less.
Up	Down	Down	We're doing our bit, Sales need to start selling. At least the cost cutting is working.

Finished Inventory	Work in Process	Cost	What's Happening and Actions
Level	Down	Down	Looks fine, no action needed.
Level	Down	Level	Looks fine, no action needed.
Down	Down	Level	Not making enough, need to increase production; at least we're keeping costs under control.

Now let's take a look from the sales organisation's point of view

Customer Service	Finished Inventory	Sales	Forecast Error	What's Happening and Actions
Down	Up	Level	Up	Don't have the right stuff. We need to get the forecasts better.
Down	Up	Level	Level	No clue, Supply making the wrong stuff? At least it's not our fault so we can carry on as is.
Level	Level	Up	Level	Great.
Level	Level	Level	Level	Great, at last those Supply guys are listening to our forecast. No need to do anything, focus on selling more.
Down	Down	Level	Level	What are those guys in Supply doing? They're going to kill us!

From these two views of the world you can see that the conclusions drawn and resulting actions are very different from each other when the view is limited.

Now let's take a look at the whole picture and see what this is telling us:

Customer Service	Finished Inventory	Work in Process	Cost	Sales	Forecast Error	What's Happening and Actions
Down	Up	Level	Level	Level	Up	Making the wrong stuff due to a bad signal from Sales. Need to fix this or use a different signal.
Down	Up	Down	Down	Level	Level	Making the wrong stuff due to "cherry picking" in production. Change the metrics to focus more on service, less on cost.
Level	Level	Down	Down	Up	Level	Great! More please!
Level	Level	Down	Level	Level	Level	Seems OK, but overall inventory going down for no apparent reason – future service problem so watch out.
Down	Down	Down	Down	Level	Level	Someone's been told to focus on cost. Need to get a better balance or there's a train wreck coming.

Now, with a broader view, we can see what's really going on. The real picture is very different from the two individual views. As a consequence, the resulting actions are different too.

In the first example, it all seems a bit trivial and obvious that we would get information from more than one place before taking action. In the second, however, while it should be just as obvious, the temptation to react to just one indicator can be very strong, particularly if there is a management spotlight on that area. In the same way as the car example ends up as a table in the troubleshooting section, we can create a play book for what to do when certain things happen. This might sound a bit dictatorial, but when you are trying to make change happen, and the right thing is counter to what people have lived with all their working lives, you need to have some very clear rules defined if you're going to get the right outcomes. All this comes down to standardised responses and the "D" word again: discipline.

In conclusion

As we can see from all this, how we measure what we are doing and the metrics we put in place are quite literally the make or break of Lean. Measure the right things and link to rewards in the right way and you will be encouraging people to focus on what's important and behave in a way that supports the process and the people who are working in it. Get this wrong, and you will end up with people pulling in different directions and working against each other. This will not only lead to poor performance, but dissatisfaction and finger pointing. Therefore, defining your suite of measures and the associated metrics is probably the most important part of your Lean success. If your process isn't quite right, or the roles and responsibilities aren't quite right, sure, there will be bumps in the road and things might get a bit hairy for a while. However, your measures will show that you're not performing to expectations and because the behaviours are right, your people will pull together to fix it. If you're sending conflicting messages from your metrics, which will cause the behaviours to be wrong, no chance! The bottom line of all this is clear: you need to set simple and visible metrics and measures that encourage the whole business, and your suppliers, to work as a team for the common good, which is delivering value to your customers. This is so obvious that it hardly needs saying here, but look around you – maybe it does need saying!

7

LEAN VS. SIX SIGMA

I couldn't leave this book without a word on the ongoing debate that still exists between your average Lead and Stat Head. Just how do Lean and Six Sigma work together? In this chapter we will look at the origins and the mindset of both and explore where the relative strengths, weaknesses and synergies lie.

Historically, there were two distinct camps here promoting solutions for improving performance. By the late 1990s, the realisation that there was a lot of common ground started to manifest itself and so, from the mid-2000s, many were promoting Lean Sigma, a blending of the two ideas into a single method. Is all of this real or is it just another marketing campaign from the consultant community trying to enhance their service offering portfolios? In this case, I think not.

In my view, they are not a single method but clearly distinct from each other. However, because of this difference they are very compatible, and both working together are essential to the success of any improvement programme. The reason they are compatible is simply that they approach the same desired outcome but from different perspectives, taking on aspects that the other can't deliver easily. Let's take a look at a brief comparison of the two from a few different angles.

Basis for change

Lean – *Trust me I know what I'm doing.* .. (hmm. .. I've heard that somewhere before)

versus

Six Sigma – *The data prove that...*

Now, if you are a Lean head, please don't take too much offence from the statement above. I know we're not all gun-slinging mavericks walking into people's businesses and changing things without a thought for the potential consequences. However, there is a distinct mindset difference at play here. Lean is a quite intuitive approach; it is based on the practitioner being able to just "see" where the issues and waste are from experience and having a brain "wired for Lean". Of course, there are tools and models to support the change hypothesis and prove the case to a degree, but it's still all a bit woolly and requires a bit of a leap of faith to get started. However, once on the road it all becomes quite obvious and the benefits start rolling in. But to motivate the leaders of an organisation to get behind a programme based on this can be a bit of a hard sell. When challenged, everyone knows instinctively that it's the right thing to do, but the finance guys tend to want a solid cash-driven business case, clearly stating where the benefits are, how much and how they will be delivered in minute detail; well, some degree of detail anyway. This is where Lean can start to fall apart somewhat, in that it is very often hard to nail down exactly where and how the cash will be delivered at the level of detail wanted. All of this makes it hard for the responsible person to commit funds and resources to something they can't quite put their finger on, particularly as it's their head on the block if it all goes pear-shaped. As a result, many Lean programmes never get off the ground and stay as localised initiatives which, as I've mentioned before, fall way short on delivery. Another thing about Lean is that it tends to be a recipe, not a menu, and all the parts need to be there in order to get the sustainable change; if one part is missing, the whole thing can start to unravel quite quickly. It's like trying to make a cake without the eggs; it just doesn't turn out right. This again makes it difficult to get agreement, as resources will always be in short supply and there will be a tendency to "cherry pick" the high-value parts and neglect the rest, with the aforementioned results. We will come back to this issue again in the chapter on business cases.

Six Sigma, on the other hand, with its roots in statistical analysis, is totally data-driven and managed through a structured method that ensures consistency and rigour. Each project is nicely bounded, has a clear objective, path to get there and a rock solid business case from the start. Therefore, a Six Sigma-based programme can be launched on the basis of X teams, delivering Y projects a year, delivering on average $Z per project, resulting in megabucks in the bank after a couple of years. This approach is a CFO's dream and will result in instant approval and application of resources to the cause.

OK, so far it looks like Six Sigma definitely has the edge over Lean. In fact, given all this, why has Lean even lasted so long, given it's all just smoke and mirrors? Indeed a paradox, but let's look from a different angle.

Incremental vs. transformational

By its very nature, Six Sigma is project-based with clear boundaries and timelines. As a result, the Six Sigma approach tends to be applied to specific issues with clear expectation for the outcomes. Consequently, Six Sigma projects provide point solutions through carefully chartered projects, delivering effective and reliable continuous improvement; solving problems with the way you do business today.

Lean, on the other hand, takes a more holistic view, looking at end-to-end processes and finding ways to do things differently, not just better. Lean, when applied beyond the shop floor, can provide the basis for a complete transformation of your business. It allows you to step out of today and into a new future, very different from what you are doing today. Lean takes a zero-base view. What does this mean? Well, it implies that your starting point is an assumption that nothing is needed. From this start you build the new way of working, adding in only what is absolutely necessary to achieve the end goal. Hang on, that sounds familiar. Cast your mind back to the very start of this book, the definition of Lean. I'd hate you to lose your place looking for it, so I'll repeat it here, plus I did say at the time that I'd be coming back to it:

"Doing the absolute minimum necessary to get the desired result."

It's fair to say that I've been in situations too many times where good people are working hard to improve a process that, when you apply the thinking above, actually wasn't needed at all. If viewed harshly, people were busy finding a way to waste their time more efficiently. It's this challenging mindset that sets Lean, or I should say, Lean Thinking, apart from Continuous Improvement Thinking, but more of this later when we look more closely at the Lean Mindset in Chapter 8.

So what's the answer? Who's right? In reality, it's not a competition; both are extremely valuable sets of tools and concepts when applied in the right circumstances. If you look more closely at the tools and approaches, you will find a high degree of commonality. Both Lean and Six Sigma have their place, either independently or side by side. It is quite legitimate to use the term Lean Sigma in cases where both are at play together as long as you don't walk away with the idea that this is somehow a third and different approach. Lean Sigma is the blending together of the two ways of thinking to enable a wide range of business issues to be addressed. In the next section we discuss where you should start; after all, it shouldn't be a random choice.

What comes first, Lean or Six Sigma?

That is a very good question and one for which, unfortunately, my consultancy background will raise its ugly head and provide the answer that every good consultant practises every day in the mirror: "It depends." In reality, this answer is not quite as frivolous as it sounds. If you think about some of the things mentioned in this book so far, the answer starts to make a bit more sense. In truth, your starting position will dictate what the priorities are, and what you need to do. As mentioned before, variation is enemy number one for a good Lean environment, so you probably need to sort this out first, at least to some extent. On the other hand, if you are consistently failing to meet delivery deadlines and have huge amounts of work in progress sitting around, then you might want to do a bit of "Leaning" first. And of course there is a full spectrum of scenarios between these two. Figure 4 sums up the idea here quite well.

What you'll notice here is that both end up in the same place, applying both as part of a continuous improvement programme once you get the initial house in order. Indeed, nearly all companies I have worked for over the years have quite rightly ended up here, with a combined "Continuous Improvement", "Operational

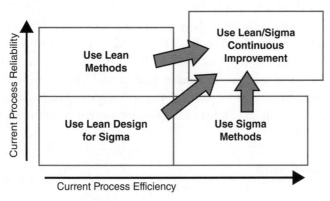

Figure 4 Lean vs. Six Sigma Starting Point

Excellence", call it what you will, programme to build on the progress made at the start. As a footnote, this realisation that there is real value in both has to come from within as experience and maturity in the thinking advances.

The other thing you'll notice is that, like in any quadrant chart, there is the lower-left box. The place no one wants to be or wants to admit they are in. In this case, being here means that whatever it is that you are doing, you're not doing it very reliably or efficiently. Not a good place to be! In essence, you're so far off track that just "Leaning" it or "Six Sigma-ing" it, won't get you very far and the only solution is a "do-over". This means rethinking and redesigning your entire approach from scratch using a combination of Lean and Six Sigma concepts to build a new way on a much stronger foundation. This unfortunate state of affairs is unlikely to apply to your entire business, but I'll guarantee that it will apply to some areas if you're really honest. A bitter pill to swallow, particularly if it's your patch. Of course, this "do-over" approach is not necessarily always a result of an existing "basket case" process or product. If you are embarking on a new area of business or have a new product to develop and bring to market, this is the obvious way to do it. Start thinking and designing with the view of not building in waste or opportunities to get it wrong from the get-go. This is why, in the chart above, this quadrant is called "Use Lean Design for Six Sigma". This sounds very obvious, but look at how you go about this in your own world. Are you thinking this way from the start? Really? Probably not entirely. The companies that do, tend to get their new products to market quicker and with fewer teething problems than those that don't. Also, for reasons I can't quite put my finger on, they seem to come up with more innovative ideas too.

In conclusion

To sum up, the main message you should take from this chapter is that it's not an either/or answer to the question. There is no real competition between Lean and Six Sigma, the "my tool's better than your tool" syndrome really doesn't apply. Lean and Six Sigma are both valuable sets of tools and ways of thinking to help you transform and improve your business at both a tactical and strategic level. The two methods are entirely compatible and, if applied appropriately at the right time, will enhance the effectiveness of each other. In this case, one plus one really does equal three. Eventually, you will end up using both; the proportions of each and the timing will depend on your priorities and capabilities at the time.

One final note here before moving on to the next chapter. There will almost certainly be one or two hard line Lean or Six Sigma people out there who will need a few gentle nudges to get them to accept the other on equal terms. Do just that: gentle nudges, not sledgehammer whacks, as these people are highly experienced and know how to apply the tools in practical ways. These gurus are ultimately your finest assets on your journey, so don't give up on them.

8

THE LEAN MINDSET

This subject, the Lean mindset, has been mentioned numerous times in this book, and is of such importance that I thought it warranted a chapter of its own. Once again, it's one of those "people" aspects of Lean that can very easily be forgotten about. But can you create a Lean mindset or does it need to be out there already? How do you know if you have it, or enough of it for Lean to take hold and mature? All very good questions, which I'll try to answer in this chapter, to some extent. Once again, I don't want to mislead and suggest that you will find a right and complete answer here because I don't think there is a right and complete answer. However, while it's difficult to put into words what a "Lean mindset" is, I'll have a go and hopefully you should find some good food for thought and pointers along the way.

It's not just about what you know

If it were as straightforward as learning the tools and the underlying concepts, everyone would be doing it, since none of this is rocket science (actually rocket science isn't that complicated). All anyone would have to do is read a few books, perhaps attend a course and off you go. However, knowing the tools and concepts is one thing, being able to "see" where and how to apply them is quite another. At the risk of sounding a bit arrogant, part of it is how your brain is wired. To some it is all just common sense; to others it's a bit more difficult to get their heads around. That's not necessarily a major problem, as we will see later when we talk about "critical mass". But it does seem to be a fact of life.

One of the issues is that applying Lean does not mean simply following a formula. As the leader of one of the companies I worked with said, "The tools and concepts are simple and consistent; however, every application is unique." She "got it", by the way. She understood that in every part of her business, the issues and demands being placed on it were different, which required different solutions with different priorities. That meant that the application of the Lean tools needed to be adapted to suit the particular situation, the "one-size-fits-all" approach just doesn't work. Being able to see how the tools can be applied and need to be adapted is critical. It doesn't stop there either. Being able to see all this and even being able to implement it won't make it work. You have to be able to communicate what you are doing and how it works to the people who are going to have to live with it and get them involved in the solution. Being able to do this is quite a different skill set. I remember one very vivid example of this from one of the companies I worked at. The person in question was absolutely brilliant; he had an unrivalled understanding of Lean and how to apply it instinctively to just about any environment. Unfortunately, he had a really hard time interacting with others and just wanted to be left alone to design and implement the solutions himself. Once done, he would present his latest baby to the world and get so frustrated that most people weren't blown away and eager to adopt his new way. As a result, some of the most logical and elegant Lean solutions that I have ever seen never got off the ground and he ended up moving on from the company. So, as the title of this section suggests, it's not just about what you know.

Lean critical mass

Will everyone in your business have that clear and focused Lean mindset, able to see all the waste as if sprayed with red paint, then instantly know what to do to remove it? Probably not, and indeed it's not even desirable for everyone to be a Lean guru. I'm sure you've heard the saying "too many cooks" and all that. What is important, however, is that you have a "critical mass" of people who do get what it's all about and who can show the rest the way forward. Again, all very nice fancy words, but what is this "critical mass" and how do you know when you've got it?

Lean critical mass is about having enough people in the right places with a balance of the key skills to make a change to Lean ways of working possible. Lean understanding in an organisation falls into three main groups. These are:

- Principal thinkers – People who have an in-depth understanding not only of the tools and concepts, but also how they can be applied to a diverse range of situations. In addition, principal thinkers have clarity on direction and the business end game, and can provide the visionary element to enable them to influence at all levels of an organisation and drive change. These people do tend to be "Lean wired", as mentioned earlier, but it's not a prerequisite.
- Practitioners – People who have a deep understanding of the tools and concepts and how to apply them. They can lead projects and change events, train others on the tools and be the game keepers for the fledgling ideas as they start to develop. Some of these will have the potential to graduate to Principal thinkers in time.
- Lean aware people – These people are easy and quick to train, get the ideas and can practise them in their own roles once on board. They are highly valuable in Lean process design workshops and in seeding the new ways of working in the organisation.

I want to make one thing absolutely clear about the above three groups before moving on. There is no actual or implied hierarchy or value rating here. Each of the above groups plays a vital role in the success of Lean. They are just different, that's all. Now we've got that out of the way, how many of each do you need? A very good question, and one that is very difficult to answer, as there is no magic formula. But let's have a go, based on a real example I was involved in recently where the company wanted to know if it had enough Lean savvy to make it work. It won't be exactly right of course, but at least it will give you an idea.

Let's take your average marketing company offices and run a few numbers to get the impression of the place. It provides three major service types using three very different processes, each with its own equipment and teams. There is a shared IT and graphics team serving all three areas. There is a large quality group responsible for customer service and quality assurance. Work and capacity planning and scheduling are carried out at a high level by the senior staff and at a detail level by the service leads in each area. There is a strong innovation team supporting all areas coming up with new and innovative ideas in terms of new markets and methods of capturing the hearts and cash of the public. HR and Finance are also shared services and the board is a leadership team of four people. All in all there are 150 people working in the business.

When we did the assessment with them, we came to the conclusion that they were just about OK, given the following results:

- Principal thinkers – There were about four of these people spread throughout the firm. Only one was on the leadership team, but that's OK. Of the others, one was a service lead in one of the areas, one was a graphics technician and the remaining one was in the innovation group.
- Practitioners – The innovation team was the obvious target here and we were not disappointed; we found three in here, 50% of the team. We also identified about another eight people dotted around the organisation that were sufficiently clued up that they qualified as practitioners in our books. One of these was on the leadership team.
- Lean aware – Here things are a little thin on the ground but just about OK. Doing a quick sample of observations and questions, we felt that there were about 15 others spread throughout the

organisation who got it enough to be able to be left to do their thing and coach others in the workplace as well as get involved in improvement project work. Again, one was on the leadership team.

As you can see, only about 20% of the total workforce fell into the above three groups. Given that there is a reasonable spread across the organisation and there is not a huge resistance to Lean as a whole, we believed at the time that this company was good to go and that its Lean transformation would proceed reasonably well, with the right support from the rest of the board. Indeed, we went back a year later and good progress was being made. In addition, the numbers in the Practitioner and Lean aware groups had risen significantly.

The most important area where having this critical mass is essential is in your leadership. While, as mentioned above, it's not necessary for all the leaders to be totally up to speed and be serious Lean thinkers; it is vital, however, that enough of the leaders are both clued up enough to understand what is going on and humble enough to listen to others who are better wired for Lean than they are. In the case above, you can see how this worked out for them. Remember that being a leader does not equate to being on the leadership team or vice versa! Now all this talk about leaders leads us nicely to the next section in this chapter.

Lean leadership

This might sound like leadership on a minimalistic level, but it's not. In fact, it is one of the most critical parts of any change programme. Good leadership will make or break the capability for any organisation to succeed. This is not news, I hear you say, and indeed this is true. But leading in a Lean culture is a bit different to the norm; not radically different, but different.

If you read all the leadership literature it's all about inspiring people to go the extra mile for the cause, whatever the cause might be.

In Lean, this is no different. Having leaders who can communicate and inspire is just as important, if not more so. The difference is in what they need to inspire. Part of this is being sufficiently clued up to understand the messages they need to give. I've seen, so many times, months of hard work unravel in a heartbeat with a few inappropriate words from a senior leader. When tackled about it, in 99% of cases, the leader in question meant no harm and didn't realise that they had given the wrong impression.

Success in Lean leadership is about instilling the right mindset, staying the course and having the right conversations. Most of all it's about understanding that getting lean is about change: changing ways of working; changing what's measured; changing what you've been doing for the last 15 years or more; but most of all, changing behaviours. All this doesn't just happen on its own, it takes leadership, but the leaders are also subject to all this change. They're not immune to the concerns and uncertainty that come with change, but leaders need to hold true to the principles and demonstrate their commitment. This is easy when things are going well, but any change worth doing will not be a walk in the park all the time; there will be problems, there will be times when the doubts that you're doing the right thing start to raise their ugly heads. This is just the time when the organisation looks to its leaders for reassurance and guidance. If the leaders start to waiver, then you've got a problem.

Being able to inspire this confidence means that leaders must believe in, not just be "OK" with, the new ways of working. This, in turn, means that leaders need to invest time to get to grips with exactly what the changes are and what they mean to the business. They also need to understand what could go wrong, how the Lean environment works in these situations and how to react when it happens, and believe me it will happen. There's nothing like a good crisis to test the true mettle of the leadership. Their behaviour, when it looks like it's all going to go bang, is make or break time. If they don't really understand at a detailed level how the Lean business works, then their reaction will probably be to revert to norm and if that happens, moving forward from there will be a very steep uphill journey.

OK, we've talked a bit about how leaders need to cope with the change. Hopefully, this will only be a transition period while confidence in the new ways builds. However, there's more to it than just leading through the change. Leading in a lean environment is different, even when it's more established. So how is it different? The following few paragraphs give an overview of some of the aspects of Lean that are vital for success and which leaders need to champion through direction, coaching and, most importantly, demonstration through their own behaviours.

Discipline

This is number one. Lean only works if the rules are well developed and everyone sticks to the rules. That means everyone: the executives don't get a "get out of jail free" card just because of who they are. In fact, it is even more important that they abide by the rules than everyone else, as they have to lead by example. Discipline means following the process as designed; if the process doesn't work then fix it, don't work around it.

Leadership vs. management

This is subtle, but it's important to know the difference. Lean is managed by good processes, visual controls and people knowing what to do depending on the signals the process and visuals are sending them. Typically, a management role is to understand what needs to be done and tell staff what to do. While there will always be a bit of this to do, the traditional role of a manager is almost redundant in a Lean world for the reasons above, but not quite. By contrast, a leadership role is to make sure everybody understands the mission, is equipped to carry it out and steps in to give practical and moral support when it's needed. Notice that this is support to help the person do their own job, not do the job for them.

Knowing the difference between accountability and responsibility

This links with the last point made above and, again, is sometimes misunderstood or not practised by those in leadership positions. The main difference is that you can, and indeed should, delegate responsibility to others if they are better equipped to carry out the task, but you can never delegate accountability. If you are accountable, it doesn't matter who actually did the deed: the buck stops with you.

Consistency

If discipline is number one, consistency must run a very close second. In reality this leadership trait is not confined to Lean and should be present in all leadership environments. In this context, however, we are talking more about staying the course, and holding true to the principles; clearly articulating what is expected and not deviating from it.

Engagement

Engagement is probably another overused word in consultant-speak. What I mean by this is that the leaders need to be in touch with the real world, understand what is expected and the problems people face on a day-to-day basis. Leaders need to show that they care about the process, the outcomes and the people doing the work. That means getting out there, seeing and hearing for yourself what's going on and being prepared to act decisively if there is a need to intervene. It also means asking the right questions. Very easy to say; not always easy to do.

Asking the right questions

Firstly, just the fact that you ask questions rather than giving orders is a good solid step in the right direction. But assuming that you are asking questions, in order to ask the right questions, you actually need to know the right answers before you ask them. Huh? Well, in a Lean world, most of the information you need as a leader is already available to you without asking, so you're not asking questions to get information. You're asking questions to drive the right behaviours and to get people to question themselves, the answers to which, of course, you already know. Things like:

"What does the process say needs to be done?"
"What is this telling you?"
"What do you think?"
"Can you explain why this is happening or why we are doing this?"

It's all about getting others to think. The other key thing about all this is that, as a leader, you need to make sure you are thinking too and asking your questions for the sake of the bigger picture; which brings me on to the next topic.

Process thinking

Process thinking is about understanding that any situation is a result of many connected cause, effect and feedback systems working together; a bit like butterflies and hurricanes but not so drastic. Let's take a real life business example.

We could take a local view and optimise the operating efficiency of a piece of equipment by running it flat out for long periods of time. On the face of it this is great, output is high, return on the equipment is high and everything is rosy. However, when you look at the bigger picture, it might not be such a smart idea. Rate of wear increases exponentially with speed, so by backing off the speed a little, the equipment would last twice as long, or have far fewer disruptive breakdowns. Add to this that the downstream process can't keep up and you don't need all that stuff anyway. When you look at it like this, running flat out doesn't seem quite such a bright idea now, does it? By slowing down a bit, the flow of the end-to-end process and consumption are in balance and you save money on repair bills.

So from this, you can see that by looking at the end-to-end process and seeing how to optimise for the whole rather than the part, you get a better result while minimising the overall effort, and what is Lean again? Achieving the desired result with the minimum of effort!

Transparency and visibility

I'm sure you've heard this one before: "Information is power". Many companies work like this; by keeping some knowledge to yourself and using it judiciously you can gain advantage over the rest. In a Lean world where being able to react to changing environments and always knowing the current status is vital, "information is power" thinking is a short road to disaster. In Lean, open access to relevant information is everything; it allows people to make decisions faster and eliminates the dependency on one person to have all the answers. The Lean leader makes information available and visible to those that need it. In addition, lean processes are based on visual controls where the current status can be seen at a glance without the need to ask or get reports created.

Of course, this does not mean that everyone needs to know about everything. There will always be some things that are on a need-to-know basis or irrelevant to a particular group. However, if it is relevant to the job, the information should be readily available.

I know this all sounds a bit like motherhood and apple pie and I make no excuses for that. This really is the essence of Lean leadership and every leader, be they a leader through rank and seniority or through peer influence, needs to interpret all this into their own roles in their own business, then consistently demonstrate it. If this happens then, over time, Lean will become the new norm for how the company works, part of the DNA of the business.

Certification?

Ah, to certify or not to certify, that is the question.

We're talking here about testing people's competency in using the tools and recognising their skills with a formal stamp of approval, not the other type of certification!

Most people like to have some letters after their name or a nice plaque on the wall. Also, having an industry-recognised certification on your CV can do wonders for your career. So, on this basis, setting up a certification programme for Lean seems like a good idea, yes? In all seriousness though, there are real benefits to having a formal mechanism to train people in the whys and wherefores of Lean other than personal gain for the people concerned:

- Ensuring that everyone is equipped with a consistent set of tools, for one thing. I've witnessed real bafflement and much throwing up of arms from people when they are visited by two or more "Lean Experts" professing the way forward, which turns out to be seemingly different directions, with different priorities and using different tools. In reality, if you dig under the surface of what they are actually saying, they will not be too far apart, just coming at it from slightly different directions. If you are one of these "Lean Experts", you can probably see this and not get too concerned about it. However, if you are the recipient of this advice, and are not totally in the know, it can all get very confusing and become a real turn-off.
- Knowing who within your organisation has been trained to what level and, more importantly, has experience in using the tools in a real situation is very useful. It allows you to create realistic

plans knowing that you have the right skills available to make your programme successful.

• Contributing personal capital to people who have committed to training and delivering real benefit to the business by awarding a recognised certification is quite simply the right thing to do.

OK, so with all this in favour of certification to underpin your Lean change, it's a no-brainer right? After all, most of the major companies doing Lean and Six Sigma have one, what more is there to say?

Ah, not so fast. When you look under the skin of a lot of companies' efforts and which have such certification, there tends to be a common issue. Most start off with good intentions, with the ideas above front and centre. However, as things progress, an unfortunate metamorphosis happens. The certification starts to take on a life of its own, becoming the end in its own right, rather than the means to an end.

Because the certification process requires specific experience and project work to be completed within a reasonable time, projects are set up specifically to qualify for certification. While the needs of the business are obviously not ignored, there can be conflict of interest when there are not-so-sexy projects that need doing, which might not be fully aligned with getting certification. I have seen this happen many times over the years at a number of very prestigious global companies. In a lot of cases, metrics are devised that report and promote certification. Numbers of certified people in the organisation now have targets, which leaders are held accountable for. The success of the programme is linked directly to achieving the target certification numbers.

This is not meant to be a total indictment of certification programmes, and if I've left you with that idea it was not intended. However, if you are going to journey down this path, please be aware of the pitfalls and ensure that you manage it carefully. If you can do this, then please go ahead.

5S as a foundation for Lean

While other Lean tools contribute greatly to the success, in terms of setting the foundation for a Lean mindset, 5S is worthy of a mention here. In this section I'm not going to give a blow by blow account of the origins and details of 5S. This will be covered to some extent in a later chapter on tools. Here, the emphasis is on the mindset and the role 5S plays in that. However, to do this, I do need to give some insight into what it is all about.

Firstly, what are the 5Ss? Here is where the confusion starts. There's more than one definition, but here is the primary one. Initially devised in Japan, the Ss are defined as follows:

Seiri	Sort, clearing, classify
Seiton	Straighten, simplify, set in order, configure
Seiso	Sweep, shine, scrub, clean and check
Seiketsu	Standardise, stabilise, conformity
Shitsuke	Sustain, self-discipline, custom and practice.

And for completeness, some companies add a 6th (6S) of Safety, although in my opinion this should be an integral part of the other steps of 5S and not a separate stage in itself.

Very simply, 5S was devised to determine an organisation's approach to its business and to evaluate its workplace organisation capability and visual management standards. It is not just about housekeeping, but concentrating on maintaining the standards and discipline.

This last word, discipline, provides the clue to the value 5S brings to the party from the Lean mindset perspective. In order to consistently rate highly in 5S, everyone in the organisation needs to respect the rules and demonstrate solid discipline in how they approach their work. In addition, as 5S is applied to a whole work area, not just an individual, 5S generates a sense of working for the team and a clear sense of ownership. All of the above are essential attributes of successful Lean. Given this, introducing 5S early can help lay a solid foundation for Lean going forward. It really is a "start as you mean to carry on" approach. Also, 5S is a part of the Lean toolset anyway, so it is certainly not a throwaway starter.

In conclusion

A Lean mindset is, to some extent, something certain people are born with, the ability to see with different eyes. However, it can be coached in most people to at least start to question their surroundings and say to themselves, "there must be a simpler way to do this". This, combined with a good knowledge of some core tools and techniques, will take you a long way on the journey. However, one or two individuals in a business with the "right stuff" can't get it done. Success requires good leadership, a critical mass of people who get it to some extent and passion from the organisation as a whole.

On the subject of certification, the jury is still out for me, though I tend to advise my clients to be very careful and ensure safeguards are in place before embarking on a comprehensive certification scheme, for the reasons outlined above. For an individual, however, it is definitely a good idea to get "belted".

9
THE DREADED BUSINESS CASE!

There's no getting away from this one, sooner or later your "... trust me, I know what I'm doing... " line will fail to carry the necessary weight to get the commitment you need to get things done. Someone will ask you to back up the claims with some hard numbers: the dreaded business case. In this chapter we look at the various types of business case, some common problems associated with them and a few tips to try to avoid them.

Business case, benefits case, case for action, best guess, what?

First things first: when the question comes, as it surely will, you need to establish what EXACTLY you are being asked for. This might sound like a stupid statement to make and you may consider it a bit of an insult to your intelligence, but you would be surprised how often the asker and the doer part company with a totally different understanding of what the outcome should be. I myself have fallen into this trap with very painful results! Presenting your high-level case for action to a confused-looking executive team to be told after you've finished, "... very good, but where's the detail, who has signed off on it, how does it link with the detailed projects? ... ". Oops!

The first thing to do is to find out what the "xxxxxx" case is going to be used for and who is asking for it. Next, go see that person and ask the same question, even if it's the CEO. Especially if it's the CEO! Understand what level of detail is needed and why, who needs to agree with it before it's presented and what should be included. Here are a few examples I've come across in my time:

> The "Financial Justification" Case – "What, realistically, is this going to deliver and how much will it cost? Give me the P&L, Balance Sheet and Cash Flow impact of the programme."

> The "Kick in the Backside" Case – "Give me a ballpark view by department what is possible so I can tell this lot they need to get their act together and stop giving me excuses."

> The "Motivational Speech" Case – "We need an overview of the benefits to the company and how it positively impacts the people so we can get everybody behind this. Err, don't make too much of a deal of the costs and negative side."

> The "Get People Bought into the New Budgets" Case – "We need everyone to understand what they need to deliver and agree to the changes in their budgets."

> The "Is it Worth Talking About" Case – "Sounds like a good idea, but is there really anything in it for us?"

All of these were called business cases by the people asking for them but the outcomes and the approaches were very different. Let's take a brief look at each to make the point a bit clearer.

The financial justification

OK, let's start with the real thing, the proper business case: a balanced, structured view of the expected benefits and costs. It is usually overseen by Finance, or at least should be! If you find Finance are taking a back seat, you need to go and dig them out and get them on board, because at the end of the day they need to sign off that the financial "rules" of the company have been applied properly. Also, having the nod from Finance keeps the " ... ah yes, but have you considered ... ", or " ... I don't agree with the way you've handled that part ... " brigade at bay.

This requires a fairly in-depth review of all the potential benefits and costs, allocating them to the right high-level chart of accounts, and applying discounting over an agreed number of years to come up with the usual financial justification ratios and numbers: Net Present Value; Return on Capital and/or Investment; impacts on Profit and Loss and Balance Sheet. In addition, there are the "soft" benefits to estimate, like customer service or satisfaction, capital avoidance, safety, compliance with laws or regulations, employee satisfaction, and so forth.

Usually this means developing some kind of model that allows the various variables to be analysed and "what-if" scenarios tried out. In most cases, you will be asked to provide some indication of impact on the organisation in terms of head count change, and a high-level milestone plan linked to the benefits' delivery and costs.

A business case of this type will usually require at least three scenarios (best, most likely and worst), a list of assumptions made and information about where the data came from. Although it will take a few iterations to get right, once in place it has real advantages: a solid base on which to set future targets and budgets; a useful tool to use for tracking the progress against plan; and a clear mandate to get the resources needed to make it happen.

This is a lot of work to prepare, get right and validate with the right people. Don't underestimate the effort, financial skills and time needed to do this. Also, don't allow yourself to be rushed. If there are gaping holes, or even little ones for that matter, the credibility of the whole thing will be questioned.

The kick in the backside

Usually prompted by C-level executives to "motivate" their teams to step up and take responsibility for delivering the maximum, this is a very different animal to the case above. The level of deep analysis is much lower and will rely more on external benchmarking, your own experience and gut feel for what is possible. It's an aspirational goal, not a balanced view.

This will be focused more on the benefits than the costs and be aligned more towards the organisational responsibilities rather than the financial chart of accounts. Buy-in on this is not usually required, which is a good thing as the outcomes will usually ruffle a lot of feathers. Agreement usually comes from around the conference table after some serious debate and bargaining, which you may or may not be invited to.

The warning here is that there will be some degree of political wrangling and finger pointing and you might become a target for a large part of this, as you put the plan together in the first place. Key to your health here is to ensure that you have the unwavering and vocal support of the senior person who is causing all the stir. It has to be very clear to all where the "kick in the backside" is coming from.

In this case, results are needed quickly; at this level, patience is a rare commodity. No need for detailed analysis here, just headlines, but they had better be right (or at least in the right ballpark) as quite a few people will have some pretty big demands made of them as a result. The results usually can be documented in the form of a presentation, providing the major buckets of benefits and some rationale for the numbers.

Don't even try to gain consensus on this one from the management team; you won't get it, nor indeed should you. If people agree with it, it's not aggressive enough. My rule of thumb to see if it's pitched about right: do a quick comfort check on what people feel is about right, then double it. By the same token, you need to have a good head to head with "The Boss" and explain in no uncertain terms that this is what is possible, not what is probable. In reality, if this has the desired effect, the actual delivery will come in somewhere around half way between this and the "comfort check" you did earlier.

The motivational speech

This is the nice one, used mainly as a "Ra-Ra" speech by the leaders! What's required here is to provide an overview of the benefits to the business as a whole. The purpose is to motivate people to get behind the cause, so no need to do a detailed analysis of hard benefits and costs here as long as the numbers kind of stack up in favour, good to go. What is important, however, is to focus on the softer side of the deal, what's in it for the people and how their lives are going to be better in the future.

Is it worth talking about?

Usually this one is done very early on, when things are very nebulous and uncertain. In some ways this is a bit like the second case, but without the animosity! All that is required is a rough estimate of the benefits and costs to allow a decision to be made to pursue it or forget it. No one should expect it to be 100% accurate, so don't try. The trick here is to quote broad ranges. If you state a single number, people will hold you to it irrespective of how many health warnings and caveats you smothered it in. One key thing: you will need a good handle on is the resource requirements, as people don't grow on trees and people will be busy doing other stuff.

The outcome you are looking for here is either "Yes, let's go and mobilise the resources", or "It's not worth the effort, there are better things to do with the people, let's move on".

Getting management bought in

Right then, up to now what we have talked about has been fairly straightforward; yes, time consuming and hard work, but straightforward. As long as the data show that everything will end up in the black rather than the red, you're fine. This one, however, is a minefield and, in most cases, a "lose–lose" situation. However, it is not unusual for this to happen and therefore it would be remiss of me not to cover it just because of my own opinion, so here goes. I got caught up in one of these and it caused me the most grief and sleepless nights of anything I have done before or since. I would also suggest, at the risk of being lynched, that it is a complete waste of time and grey hairs, as the outcome will always be so compromised and watered down that it does more harm than good in the end. To risk the rope even more, I would go so far as to say that if leadership ask for this to be done, it is a clear signal that they don't have the guts to stand up and demand real change in their own organisations and are not prepared to set stretch targets for their management teams. There, I said it; I can hear the summons letters dropping through the letterbox already. Well, there it is, I've done it. I hope my prejudices haven't come over too strongly.

Now to the task at hand! The purpose of this type of business case is to provide an understanding on what the benefits are going to be at the middle layers, then get consensus from the same group on the numbers. This involves putting together a straw model of the benefits case at quite a detailed level, followed by an extended "road show" to talk to each person, ensure they understand it and negotiate their contribution. All will be well aware that whatever number is arrived at, that same number will appear in their targets the next time they are revised. Given this, it's no wonder it's a very conservative view!

In the next section, we explore some of the potential problems you might encounter and a few tips to try and avoid them.

Some business case bear traps

A business case, whatever its purpose, is always going to be a highly visible document, usually in very high places. This puts the poor old soul who was picked on to prepare it in a very tight space and potentially open to making some very career-limiting mistakes. This section is about how to avoid the big ones and is, in many cases, delivered through bitter personal experience. So, read on.

The devil's in the detail

This is not about how detailed your business case is, but more about whether it will stand up to scrutiny and challenge. There is no better way to lose all your hard-earned credibility than by some smart devil finding an error in the numbers or the logic. The more complex or detailed the case gets, the more likely this is going to happen. The key here is to be very organised from the outset and follow a few simple rules:

- Get your information from more than one source; if there is a significant difference, do some more digging. If this fails, you will have to make an assumption (see later).
- Decide at the outset the level of detail you are going to and keep checking that you are not getting deeper and deeper as time goes on.
- Keep it as simple as possible; if there are complex algorithms or calculations involved, do it one step at a time, building up the elements individually rather than the 10,000 character formula. This allows you to check and find a problem much more easily.
- Be very methodical and consistent.

If you stick to these few simple guidelines you will stand a decent chance of avoiding these bear traps, at least the bigger ones. However, you can greatly improve your survival chances by getting help, as follows.

Firstly get someone, preferably someone who has a reputation for detail, to go through the thing from top to bottom with a fine-tooth comb. You'll be surprised how many errors this will find, even if you've been through it a thousand times.

Secondly, get a different person, preferably a more senior strategic thinker, to work through the logic of the assumptions and conclusions you are making.

Oh, and while we're on the subject, a word about assumptions. You will never be able to gather and validate all the information you need; you will have to make assumptions, better known in the outside or real world as guesses. (Funny how that term is avoided in businesses. For some reason, making assumptions sounds more professional than making guesses!) There is nothing wrong in doing this, even making big ones. The important thing is to write them down with their implications then go through them with your audience so they understand them.

Before we leave the detail bear trap, there is another aspect to this you need to be aware of. In every business case preparation I've been involved in, I've run into the "data miner". This is the person who craves every last scrap of information, who wants every last possible scenario explored to the nth degree with supporting affidavits signed in blood. You have to be very careful not to get drawn into this never-ending spiral of detail because every step you take down this road will reveal twice as many more you need to take to explain how you took the first one. You have to keep front and centre in your mind that a business case is a means to an end, not an end in its own right. Understand what the purpose is and satisfy yourself that what has been produced is fit for that purpose, then defend it. Ah, a nice way to slide into the next section.

Fit for purpose

This is a bit of a follow-on from the explanation of the different types of business case mentioned above. The issue here is how your carefully prepared and communicated business case ends up being used.

Usually it starts out all fine and dandy; you get the request, you check out what the requester is wanting to do with it, you do the work and present the outcomes. All the heads are moving up and down with smiles on them and everything in the garden is rosy. Then a few months pass and, unbeknownst to you, your carefully planned and positioned case has been doing the rounds. It's been scrutinised by the CFO, it's been taken by someone to one of the badly performing sites for the Site Leader to get red-faced over. It's been cut, edited and plagiarised in newsletters and on the intranet site. What happens next is that people's defensive instincts kick in and all that hard work in positioning it for the right message goes out the window and it gets systematically shredded before your eyes, and, more importantly, in front of everybody else's too. It is impossible to stop this from happening, but there is a bit of damage control you can do up front. The key point here is "up front". If you try to do this after the event it just sounds like making excuses for a poor job and gets you no points at all; in fact, it can make things worse. So, what can you do?

Firstly, put a clear statement in the preamble explaining the purpose of the business case and how it should be used. More importantly, you need to say in words of one syllable what it's *not* to be used for and why. This will help to some extent, but you can guarantee that this front page will mysteriously have been lost when an angry executive throws a copy at you, demanding to know what the "bleep" you thought you were "bleeping" doing. However, at least you can get out the original and start to explain.

Secondly, make sure that the person who made the request in the first place understands the potential for misuse and subsequent consequences. Get a commitment that anyone he or she passes it on to is made clear of the original purpose and is prepared to stand by it when the rocks start flying.

In my experience, neither of the above will be really effective, but it's better than nothing. In reality, a good quality suit of armour hanging on the coat hook and ready to don quickly can come in quite useful at this point.

Where are the big fish hiding?

This is all about keeping the focus on what matters at all times. By their nature, business cases are full of numbers and involve a lot of messing around in spreadsheets, charts and graphs. After two to three weeks of this, combined with endless meetings and discussions with people from all over who will have their own "degree of importance" scale, it's very easy to lose sight of the bigger picture. Yes, completeness is important but you can't put a £200 purchasing saving in the same sentence as a £500m uplift in revenue through improved service. The sources of benefits will be many and diverse and you need to sift through these and put each into some kind of context. At the end of the day, it's important to be able to articulate very clearly where the big bucks are: what are the key three or four things, which, if implemented, will make a big difference? This will get people excited a lot more than, " ... If we do this list of 500 changes, the overall benefit is X ... ". So, find the big fish and make a big shout about them, bundle up the rest into an "other stuff to do" bucket and get focused on what is really going to make the difference.

Great, now we're motoring. However, there is a big health warning which needs to be attached to this. Read on!

The cherry picker

This is the final point I have to make here in this "bear traps" section and it can have a disastrous effect on the outcomes from your beloved Lean journey. It can happen very easily on its own, but coupled with the idea above can really get some momentum behind it. It's the "Cherry Picking Syndrome". Briefly, it's this: once you start tying benefits to specific activities, particularly big ones, there will be a strong tendency for the leadership to want to do only the activities that deliver the biggest benefits and ignore the rest. On your Lean journey, this can be very dangerous, if not disastrous, as there is usually a lot of interaction going on and missing out some of the enabling activities can negate the delivery of the big ones people are getting all excited about.

An analogy I use a lot here is: "Successful, long lasting Lean change is a recipe, not a menu." On a menu you are given a selection to choose from and you pick what most appeals to you. A recipe, on the other hand, needs all the ingredients to be added in the right quantities, in the right order and in the right way to work. Imagine a sponge cake without the eggs or just thrown in the oven without being mixed!

This cherry picking is almost inevitable, particularly when you start asking for resources or money:

"You want how many people and how much money? Are you mad? What if we only do … "

This, you need to be ready for. Obviously there will always be optional parts or "nice to haves", and be prepared to give some ground here. However, be sure you understand the essentials and be prepared to defend them. Sometimes it's a hard sell, but be persistent. A "told you so" a year later when everything has unravelled doesn't really pass muster, does it?

In conclusion

The dreaded business case is an absolute pain in the proverbial, but essential if you are going to get any real traction and commitment in the end. There is nothing wrong with any of the five types of business case described above, all have their strengths and weaknesses and a role to play in getting everyone on board. The trick is to understand clearly what the purpose is and ensure you pick the right one for the particular situation you are in at the time. In many cases, you will need to do all of the above at some point, so be prepared!

10

KEYS TO SUCCESS AND SUSTAINABILITY

So far we've been focusing on the change from the old ways to new, Lean ways – understanding the concepts, understanding the potential for improvement and making the changes. This is all well and good, but if it all unravels over time, it's all for naught. Making a change is one thing, sustaining a change is quite something else, and this is where many a promising Lean programme has foundered on the rocks. While it would seem absurd to put in all that effort, just to let it all fall apart, it happens more often than not. But why does this happen? There are a number of reasons which we will explore in this chapter, along with some tips for avoiding them.

Top reasons for failure

Reason number one has to be treating the change to Lean as a project. This has a number of consequences which can put the long-term success in jeopardy.

Firstly, projects tend to be considered completed when the visible work is completed, like new processes or a new organisation. The biggest part of Lean is not the visible stuff, it's the invisible stuff. It's difficult to plan and schedule this in a project plan. It usually ends up as a couple of long bars at the bottom of a 2000-line process change plan with the titles "Change Management" and "Training". While everyone will make the right noises about the need for these, very few people really understand what these entail or the consistent effort it takes to do it.

Secondly, projects are usually done by project teams pulled out of the main business to do their thing and deliver it, completed, to the business. In the meantime, the "business" is getting on with business-as-usual. Both of these have made the assumption that there is a start and a finish to Lean; an end product to be delivered to the business on a silver platter by the team, to be accepted or rejected based on how well the team sell it. However, as we have learned throughout this book, Lean is a journey: it has a start, but doesn't end. Also, it's a journey for everyone to take together – new concepts to be understood, new ways of working the process and working with each other to adopt attitudes, and behaviours to change, some of which have been established over many years.

Reason number two is "All change!" What's the latest saying? "The only constant in life is change"? Well, it does seem to be these days, senior leaders seem to be changing jobs all the time in a constant game of musical chairs, both within their own company and between companies. These changes are then reflected in the next few layers down as the new guy or girl puts their own mark on the organisation. This constant churn and the desire for the new person to make their mark really threatens long-term change where consistency in direction is important to maintain the momentum. This does not mean that plans and expectations are set in stone; Lean is not a dogma to be pursued on an arrow-straight course no matter what. Of course, priorities change and new issues and opportunities constantly bubble to the surface and need to be taken care of, but the underlying fundamentals and drive to the Ideal State need to be consistent as all these changes are happening. If this issue is coupled with number one above, failure is almost inevitable.

Reason number three for me has to be unrealistic expectations. Now, let me be very clear here, I'm not talking about the potential benefits of Lean, as these usually surpass the wildest dreams of any sane individual, as we'll see in a later chapter. No, I'm talking here about time and effort. In the current world of instant gratification, there is little patience or consideration for the long term. Shareholders, and hence leadership, want results now, not promises of jam tomorrow. Moreover, there can be a gross misconception of the effort it takes to turn a supertanker onto a new path. The combination of lack of resources and instant delivery expectations will doom a promising Lean programme before it even gets out of the starting blocks. I've been there a few times myself.

Finally in this tale of woes we have the house-of-bright-ideas syndrome. "What?" I hear you say. Let me explain. Lean is not new; many people have read the books, even this one. Many more have experience in doing Lean somewhere or at some point in the past. There will probably be some Lean projects and activities going on already in your own neighbourhood right now. "Yes, so what?" Well, the problem here is that all these people have bright ideas about how Lean can improve their part of the world and how to do it. In most cases they are absolutely right on both counts, and therein lies the problem. Taken individually, all these ideas and methods are fine and will deliver results in their respective areas. Unfortunately, unless you are extremely lucky, in which case I advise you to take up a career playing the lottery, all these bright ideas won't join up, it will be like trying to make a picture out of 500 pieces taken from 10 different jigsaw puzzles. Not only will the pieces not fit together, the resulting picture won't make much sense either. The resulting confusion in the population at large from all these seemingly disparate approaches and priorities very often can lead to a loss of credibility for Lean as a whole. This can ultimately lead to its relegation to a nice way to make incremental improvements in local areas, rather than a means to change the world.

There are many more reasons for failure which I'm sure you can think of, but I've tried to present a few of the common ones, just to set the nature of the canvas on which you might be expected to paint your Lean journey. This might give the impression that all is lost. Is there any hope for the future and should we even bother? Well, yes, there is hope and, yes, you should bother. In the next few paragraphs I'll try to present a few tips for overcoming some of the problems expressed above. Not all will work for you, and you'll have to come up with a few ideas for yourself as well, but it might just tip the balance.

How to avoid them

As mentioned above, this is not the definitive list of solutions to the problems, neither are they a "silver bullet" to assuring success. No, there will always be risks, but here are just a few thoughts on some common and typical approaches to lessening the risk of failure.

Buy-in at all levels

While this list of hints and tips is not in any particular order, maybe this floated to the top because of its criticality. "Buy-in" is a very often used and abused term, so in this context what does "buy-in" actually mean? It means two things: understanding and commitment.

Let's start with the first of these. There has to be a clear understanding of: the goals; the vision, or Ideal State as we described in Chapter 2; the approach to get there; the time to get there and the steps along the way; and the effort needed in all quarters to achieve the goals. This means different things to different people, so this understanding needs to be tailored to suit the audience. Your average senior executive will rapidly lose interest if you start going on about the details of specific tools used in specific areas; while the people at the coal face very well might be very interested in these details as they will have to live with them. Getting this level of understanding means being able to tell a good story, and, like any good story, it will have an introduction that puts the rest of the story into context, a middle where the details relevant to the audience are laid out, including what is expected of them, and a conclusion where the benefits of adopting the new way are heralded. This story, or series of stories, needs to be repeated often at many levels of granularity using many vehicles to get the message across. The main things to remember are: keep it simple; keep it consistent; and keep it going.

With this done, we have at least a critical mass of people across the organisation understanding the "what" and the "how". Next you need to work on the "why", gaining commitment to do it. I think I've said this before here, but I'll say it again: you can't make people do something; they have to want to do it. In other words: they have to commit, you can't on their behalf. Again, this means different things to different people, so we need to be a bit more specific about what commitment you are asking for. Let's start at the top. There are three things you are looking for here: agreement on the business goals and fundamental operating principles, in other words the Ideal State; a pledge to be true to the cause for the duration in terms of messages sent out from the leaders, demonstrated behaviours and giving the Lean agenda priority over other initiatives that might come along; agreement to fund the resources necessary to do the work over the long term. Getting this level of commitment usually comes down to money; if the return on investment is higher than anything else, you'll get it. Keeping it is another matter – you'll need to keep reinforcing the message and competing with all the other issues and priorities coming at them from all sides. Senior level people seem to have the attention span of a goldfish. While Lean might be the best thing since sliced bread for them now, once the story is more than a couple of months old, it's ancient history and the next big thing is on their minds, so you need to keep the sense of urgency up, and the messages fresh. Delivering hard benefits on a continuous drip-feed basis helps quite a lot too.

Now let's go to the other end, the grass roots. This is where all the work gets done. Most people here just want to get the job done without having to kill themselves and get rid of all the frustrations that get in the way. Assuming you have done the "understanding" bit above reasonably well, getting commitment here is usually not too hard as long as you can show how life will be better in the new world and then demonstrate this in a couple of areas. Change at this level is contagious and once a few experience the new world, the grapevine starts humming with news and everyone wants a piece, assuming the feedback is positive of course! If it's not, you're dead! So make sure the early wins are just that, wins.

Now for the middle; this is the hard one, as the impression that Lean can give is that the middle layers have the least to gain and the most to lose. In some respects this might be true, but if you don't have this group with you, the messages from the top about how important this all is will not make it through, and as people tend to listen most to the direct line managers, they have a big influence on the grass roots too. So, what do you do?

The worst thing to do is to put your head in the sand and hope the problem doesn't happen, because it will. While I hate using stereotypical statements, I'm going to here, but please recognise that people are individuals and all will have different fears, ambitions and political agendas, so be ready to adapt!

Middle managers are the glue of an organisation, transmitting and interpreting the strategic goals and policies from on high to practical terms and actions needed further down by specific teams. As such, they are in a pretty precarious position, often held accountable for the successful delivery of the on-high directives. In addition, middle management is the first step into leadership for many. As a result, there are a number of considerations to take into account when trying to get buy-in to a major change from this group:

- They are very often promoted to this role due to good technical performance, not necessarily demonstrated leadership skills that they are trying to develop on the fly.
- They often feel disconnected from the change, caught between the big picture view of a new world order in the company and the detailed working of processes and procedures.
- They are usually rushed off their feet trying to juggle the multitude of priorities and minor crises (some not so minor) which plague the everyday departmental world, so time needed to understand and embrace something very new is in short supply.

- They feel the most threatened by any change. As mentioned before, this is the group which is the usual target for cost-saving initiatives, as the top guys are considered too important to cut and the grass roots can be seen to be adding value.

In order to get buy-in here you need to address at least some, if not all, of these areas. Here are a few ideas which are not necessarily targeted at a single concern area but will build on each other to tackle the whole.

The first of these is to stop talking and listen. A mentor of mine when I was starting out as a consultant many years ago gave me some advice I've never forgotten, but sometimes had difficulty practising: "God gave you two ears, two eyes and one mouth. If you can use them in those proportions, you will become a good consultant." In this context, that means that you need to understand where people are coming from, what are the concerns and fears and what's causing them. You can't do this with a PowerPoint presentation. Listening serves two purposes: it helps you understand better; it signals to the other person that you are interested in what they have to say and their concerns. This all starts to build a level of trust.

The next is helping with the understanding of the changes coming and the role they will play in them. It's not that change will happen to them, but more that they will be an agent of that change, using their understanding of the local area and the people in it to oil the wheels. They need to understand, but more importantly believe, that their role and assistance are vital to success. Obviously this is predicated on a solid communication of what the change is and how it benefits the business, otherwise it seems like change for change's sake. This communication needs to be relevant at their level, as well as to the big picture. This is all about making the connections.

Once you have a degree of understanding, there is a need to set realistic expectations. People need to know what they are expected to do and what they are expected to deliver. Giving someone a generic role in a change programme will not cut it; they need to have something concrete to hold on to as they are going to have to process and prioritise against all the other stuff on their plate on a day-to-day basis. Recognise they will need help here and that something might need to be taken off the table rather than just adding to the load.

Follow up on discussions, especially if there were some actions coming out of them, particularly yours. Keep connected and maintain the focus on the future and the steps to get there.

Finally, don't lie. Most people can tell instantly if they're being hoodwinked or manipulated. If there is bad news, don't try and cover it up, be open, honest and tell it as it is. While there might be an initial adverse reaction, at least you now have somewhere to move forward from. If it's discovered later through the grapevine that you sugar-coated the situation, it can only end badly for all concerned.

Get the fundamentals in place

In the last section, I focused on the emotional connection with the changes from the people impacted; now I want to cover the business and physical connection and engagement. Success here is avoiding overstressing the business and putting a solid foundation in place to build on. Going full bore into a transformational Lean change all at once and turning an unprepared world upside down is a bit of a risk to say the least. The first step in this foundation setting must be getting control of the environment.

Implementing Lean in an unstable environment is not ideal. That does not mean that everything has to be perfect, just reasonably predictable. What we're looking for here is some degree of repeatability, even if that repeatability is far from best practice benchmarks in terms of performance. The judicious use of a few of the Six Sigma tools can help a lot here. By getting stability you will now be able to see more clearly what needs to be done to improve, as a lot of the noise will have been removed. In addition to this, the stress level in the business will be reduced, making acceptance of the improvement work easier to get. Applying some of the more basic Lean tools like 5S and visual controls will also help to get things under control. So, the point here is, get the house reasonably in order before improving it.

Clarity of roles and responsibilities is the subject of the next one. In my experience, much of the confusion and trouble with how things flow is centred on a lack of clarity on who is responsible and accountable for what and, even worse, who should be making the decisions. Getting this straightened out and better aligned to the process should be part of the foundation. Again, once clear, further work to make it all a lot slicker can build on this. Along with this will come a set of relevant and simple metrics to keep track of what is going on and what trigger actions to take.

Another critical step to laying the foundation is to arrive at a common approach across the board. This means a common set of tools, common ways to apply them and common terminology. While this is fairly easy in a smaller company, getting everyone talking the same language, in Lean terms that is, across a multinational organisation can be a very big headache, but one that must be addressed.

The final part here is skills and capabilities. It is important that the people are properly tooled up to do business in the new ways. This is not just about training the Lean guys on the use of Lean tools and techniques, it's about making sure everybody understands the ins and outs of how the Lean business is supposed to work and the part they play in it. Lean processes and roles can be very different, and driving on too fast before everyone is up to speed will cause all sorts of false starts and problems later.

Working on the right stuff

The boundary between this topic and the one above is quite blurred really. What I'm trying to do here is to identify what to apply the foundation built above to. There are three key things to consider here, all of which build on all of the above and will set you off on the right track.

Firstly, you want to make an impact in an area that's going to be noticed. This is about managing risk as well as being bold. If you want to get everyone fired up, you need to work on something that will really make a difference, not some backwater area which most people don't even care about. What can you do that will prove the point and impact a lot of people or move the needle in a significant way on something that is important to the business? Do this and you'll really get people's attention. Obviously you'll get the attention even if it all comes crashing around your ears as well as if it is successful, just in a different way! That's why it's a balance. If you're going to be bold, which you might have to be, just make sure there is a high probability of success and even if there is, have a back-up plan just in case!

The next thing to think about is timing. As mentioned before, attention spans and patience, particularly at more senior levels, are notoriously short. Therefore, getting a few quick wins on the board early on will really help here. They don't have to be big, they don't have to be exemplars of Lean application, just there and visible. Get people involved; deliver something and make a real shout about it. There are a couple of points to make here though, which I've seen in a few cases. Firstly, one nice, quick win followed by a drought for a year or more tends to be a bit of a disappointment for all. Secondly, there's only so long you can keep banging on: "Remember that change we made back in the last century? Well there's more on the way." Once you've started, keep it coming, a little, often is the key phrase here, especially if it's in different areas. However, don't let the drive for quick wins distract from the main cause. You can't deliver transformational change through a collection of quick wins, that's Continuous Improvement.

The final tip in this section is closely linked to the one above on setting a good foundation. This is about making sure all the pieces fit together and build on each other. To take the house-building analogy a step further: when you build a house there is plan to tell you what the finished building is going to look like and what facilities it's going to have. Then there is a particular order in which things are done to ensure that everything stays up while the building is going on. This is true for Lean as well. There is the plan, the Ideal State. Then the foundation is put in place, as described above. Building on this, there will be a logical order and timing to all the other key changes that need to happen in order to arrive successfully at your "Ideal State". This is called the transformation map, or T-Map. I can't tell you exactly what this looks like or what it contains as it is unique to every case, but I can give you a clue as to how to develop it. It's a bit like a project plan, but at a much higher level, and usually is in pictorial form. The thinking follows the same logic as value stream mapping, starting at the customer, in this case the Ideal State. With a clear understanding of what this is, you need to ask the question: "What needs to be in place to deliver this?" You need to consider all aspects: process; organisation; leadership; skills; technology. There may be 10–12 key things on this list. From there you work steadily backwards from each one to the current state, identifying a series of major steps needed and when they need to be put in place. After doing this for each of your key items you will end up with maybe 50–60 time-phased activities, each one a building block for one aspect of the Ideal State. This, then, is your transformation map. Each one of the items is a project in its own right which can be started at the appropriate time in the knowledge that the prerequisites for success will be in place when it starts. This might sound a bit abstract, but let's walk through a simple everyday example.

Imagine you've just moved into a new house and have always dreamed of the perfect garden with an herbaceous border, shade for the swing chair in the corner and that perfectly green manicured lawn. That's your Ideal State. For the sake of argument, let's assume that your current state is a building site. Now let's look at what needs to be in place to get there, starting from the ideal: a tree in the corner big enough to sit under; well-prepared flowerbeds along the borders with the right plants; a flat area with a good-quality lawn and no weeds. Then we go down a level. For the sake of space let's just do one part, the herbaceous border: we'll need to select the right plants and grow them to the required size. To do this we need to have a prepared bed a year in advance and sow the seeds or plant the small plants. To prepare the bed we need to have tilled it and added good compost to a depth of 12 inches. At this point this joins up with the other legs, as the tree and the lawn all need a good, well-prepared soil as a foundation – there's that word again! You can see where this is going. Even in this everyday example, you need to consider gardening skills, the necessary discipline to keep the garden looking good and tools for the different jobs.

Figure 5 demonstrates what this might look like as a T-Map:

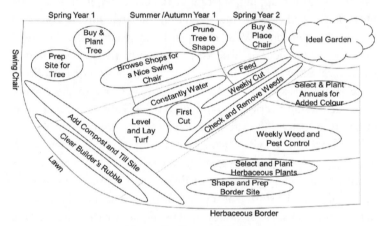

Figure 5   Example T-Map

Life doesn't stand still

One final point to remember is that life goes relentlessly on and people come and go over time. As new people come on board, they won't necessarily be on the same page. They might not know any-thing at all about Lean or might have a different view on how to apply it. If this goes on unaddressed, there is a danger that the whole thing can get diluted as more and more people change. To avoid this, you need to give some serious thought to an induction programme for new people. This doesn't have to be too big or too deep, just enough to make sure that there is a consistent understanding of what is going on and how it's all supposed to work. Some things to consider include:

- A walk through the Ideal State.
- A short overview of the change programme, what the main activities are and how they're being governed.
- An overview of some of the Lean concepts being used, where and how.

This is also a good opportunity to get some fresh ideas.

In conclusion

This has been quite a long chapter, but I make no apologies for this. If you look at the statistics, about 75% of Lean programmes fail to deliver what they were expected to, or just fade away after a couple of years. Compare this with Toyota's journey that has been ongoing and successfully gathering momentum for decades. The difference is setting off on the right foot to start with and recognising that it's more about the people than the process. One more thing to remember here is that change takes time to get used to, so don't start off with the most innovative, aka scary, part. Start off a bit smaller to get people in the mood. Once you have this, apply some of the ideas above to set a good foundation. After you've taken care of this, you can be as ambitious and as out-on-the-edge as you like, knowing that there is a good probability that it will stick.

11

A FEW KEY TOOLS

In this chapter we'll explore a few of the tools of the trade that get pulled out of the box on a regular basis. This is not an exhaustive list of all the tools available in the world of Lean and Six Sigma – that alone would fill all the space available in this entire book more than twice over. Also, I won't provide a comprehensive explanation of how each of these tools is used, so you'll have to be content with a brief explanation of what it is and what it applies to. The only exception to this is Rhythm, which I bang on about at quite some length, probably because it is really simple and very good at solving a perennial production problem, but rarely heard of and often misunderstood. A less important reason might be because I was one of the four people who thought up the idea one afternoon in a Price Waterhouse (now PricewaterhouseCoopers) office in Philadelphia back in 1996!

While a lot of the examples are more about a work environment, I've tried to relate to everyday use as well where it makes sense. So, here we go.

Diagnostic tools

In this first section I'm going to focus on some "diagnostic" tools. What I mean by that is the tools that will help you understand what is currently going on and to design the new world. Later I'll come on to the "implementation" tools, which can be used to put the new design in place, monitor it and provide the feedback to keep everything going.

5 Whys

This is a very simple technique that I'm sure most people already know about, but is surprisingly difficult to do. Why is it difficult to do? Well, you feel a bit of a pain in the backside when you keep asking "why". Why do you feel like a pain? Because it makes people feel uncomfortable if you keep digging for a more specific answer. Why do they feel uncomfortable? Because it seems like you are challenging what they do. Why do they feel as if they're being challenged? Because you don't seem to be accepting their answers. Why should this be seen as not accepting their answers? Because it just does, now go away! You get the picture of how this works and why it's hard. You'll particularly understand this if you're a parent, as small children are absolutely brilliant at doing this. Seriously though, it really is good at getting to the root of an issue and cutting through all the preconceived ideas and beliefs. If used properly, unlike the example above, once you get to the third or fourth "why" people begin to start saying "Yes, why do we do this? Perhaps we shouldn't." If not, then you will end up with a very good reason why something is as it is. The reason I've come to this one first is because it plays a very important role in using the next tool on the list properly.

Value stream mapping

One of the best tools for identifying waste and really understanding what is going on is value stream mapping (VSM). It is probably the tool I use the most when I'm wandering around a client's site poking my nose in all sorts of places to find out what's going on. Again, many books and articles cover this important tool in detail;

one of the best in my view is *Learning to See* by Womak and Shook from the Lean Institute, and I would encourage you to get hold of a copy before setting out.

As its name suggests, VSM is all about mapping the process from the point of view of delivery of value to the customer. There are two types of VSM: a current state and a future state, their names accurately reflect what they relate to. A properly constructed VSM, whatever its type, has four main components:

1. The process flow – this is the sequence of steps that whatever process you are mapping goes through to reach the customer. It will start with the customer and end with a supplier or suppliers. The level of granularity you need will depend on what it is that you are using it for, but the rule of thumb for a current state map is keep drilling down until you get a clear understanding of what is going on so that you know what you need to do to improve it. One important thing to remember is that inventory locations, whether planned or unplanned, need to be on the map, usually depicted as triangles.

2. The data boxes – under each process step there is a data box that records relevant data about the process, such as batch sizes, capacity, staffing levels, process yields, amounts of inventory, and so on. The most important data element here is the cycle time (not to be confused with the lead time!); this is the time it takes to process one unit of whatever it is that you are doing at that step. The reason for this will become clear later.

3. The information flow – this shows what information is needed at each step and where it comes from. As a minimum it should be clear where the signal to do something and what to do come from, be it a weekly schedule or demand trigger or whatever. Normally, you provide some indication of how that signal is arrived at as well, such as a forecast. You may even want to identify which systems are used for what information.

4. The timeline – this is the final part, which in fact is one of the most important parts and where the "V" comes from in the

name. It is the last thing you do and looks like a step function, with a step down as the line passes under each process step. The top part is the non-value-adding time; the bottom part is the processing time, which is the cycle time for each of the steps. It doesn't stop here; of the process time, only a small fraction is value adding. In 99% of cases, the non-value-adding time is almost equal to the total elapsed time or lead time for the process. It is this part that blows most people away when they realise that 95%+ of the time something is "in-process" – it's just sitting there waiting and not having any value added to it at all; in fact, it's collecting waste!

Visually, this is demonstrated in Figure 6.

The following example is for a mortgage lender loan application and approval process and is a real case. As you can see, out of 16 days of elapsed time, only 36 minutes are value adding; not an unusual situation for any example, but quite shocking really.

So, how do you go about creating a current state VSM? I gave you a clue when I mentioned about poking my nose in to all kinds of places. The answer is you need to go and look, observe, ask questions and make sure you're not being fobbed off with the stock "well, it was designed to work like this… " answer. Ask the people doing the work, go to the place they're doing it and give them your best sceptical look until they cave in and tell you what's really happening. One tip here is: if you're being walked through it in a conference room by someone showing you slides, it's probably so far from the truth that it's useless for what you need it for. Look everywhere too, you'll be surprised how many hidden branches and workarounds you discover when you really start digging beyond the surface. It's these hidden treasure troves that are the key to finding the waste. Anecdote time! I remember one place I went to where, after about a day of snooping around and asking awkward questions, I finally arrived at a storeroom door, which my guide was about to guide me right past. I stopped him and asked: "So what's in there?" He looked a bit sheepish and finally relented and told me

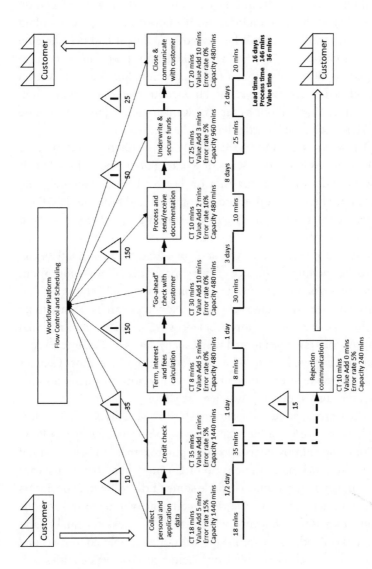

Figure 6 Example of a Value Stream Map

that this was where all the rejects of the line were put until they could be reworked. "Can I have a look?" I asked. Very reluctantly he unlocked the door and showed me floor to ceiling racks stuffed full of rejected product. When asked how long it had been here he said "about a year". When we looked into it we found it represented about two months of full production. So, don't be ushered past closed doors! Unless it has a hazardous material warning on it, of course. That's about as far as I want to go on the current state VSM, so let's spend a little time on the future state.

The future state VSM needs a little more attention to detail as it will define what the new ways of working are going to look like. It also provides the basis for a lot of the cost benefits you are going to claim. Therefore, it needs to be complete and presentable. All the parts are the same as for the current state VSM, so there is no need to repeat them here. So let's get straight to how you create one. The first real difference is that you and you alone can't do it, unless you have the undying confidence of everyone that you know more about everything than everyone else combined. Very unlikely, so let's go with: you need to engage the people. Now there are two ways to go at this: the continuous improvement way, or the transformational way. As the transformational way usually starts at a high-level concept, this is more like an "Ideal State" definition (remember Chapter 2?) than value stream mapping, so we'll ignore this here. So how does the continuous improvement way work?

The starting point is the current state VSM. This is best if it's like wallpaper covering a big wall – the last thing you want is a PowerPoint slide at this stage. Next you pull together a mixed group of people to work on it; there is no "right mix" here, but as a starter for ten, you might want to include some of the following: operators or people actually doing the work, someone who plans it, someone who supervises it, someone who tests it or checks for quality and a couple of others. Also, if you know the people concerned and can pick and choose a bit, you want a mix of personalities too: the visionary; the sceptic; the picky; and the organiser. Doing this will ensure that you enter into the situation with the best chance of coming at it from many directions, getting some fresh ideas, which will get kicked around for robustness a few times.

Next, you need to work through the map on the wall from customer end to supplier end, and go down every branch, nook and cranny and ask some serious questions.

The first question is: "Is this adding any value and can we stop doing it?" This is a tricky one, as initially you'll get the "of course it does and of course we do" response. But be persistent and use the "5 Whys" approach mentioned above to really challenge the thinking. Always start from the premise that something isn't needed until someone proves that it is.

If the above doesn't result in the whatever-it-is being crossed out, the next question is: "Can this be done better?" Well, the answer should always be "yes" but let's be realistic and add the caveat "in a reasonable amount of time and with a reasonable amount of effort" to the question, which should thin things down a bit. If so, you don't actually need to define the detailed "how" at this stage, just identify that there is an opportunity which needs to be followed up on and a very brief expectation of what an improved version might work like. Once you've done this, you end up with a new VSM that incorporates the changes and a list of projects to implement it.

Now, the purists will say that a VSM needs to be complete and have all the data elements in place and drawn to the standards, but I must confess that in my case this is not very often how mine end up. True, if I'm presenting back assessment results or working with an improvement team on a future state VSM, I'm a bit more thorough and professional about it, particularly for the future state maps. However, if I'm using it to quickly record what I'm seeing and to organise my own thoughts, a quick sketch of the process, data about the really key points and a rough timeline give me what I need. I think that it is this flexibility that makes this tool one of the most useful in the box and why it's number one on my list.

Root cause analysis

This is surprisingly hard to do, as it goes a little against normal human nature. For most of us, our brains are wired to process information and draw "gut feel" conclusions quickly, then act. This isn't surprising when you consider where we came from. If a hungry lion appears at your cave entrance, you need to be able to recognise the problem, determine a course of action and act in a few seconds, or die. There wasn't the time to sit down and analyse the situation and consider all possible actions before doing something. But serious root cause analysis requires just this, the relentless pursuit of the truth and a bit of Mr Spock Vulcan logic. It's amazing how often really bright people give in to their basic human nature too soon and jump to a conclusion when not all the evidence has been considered or points to that conclusion. Every miscarriage of justice that has gone through our legal system is a testament to this. Someone, somewhere along the line made the facts fit the gut feeling or ignored a fragment of evidence which didn't quite fit.

Many of the tools in use here are equally at home in both diagnosis and implementation, and there are a lot of them. Given this, I was a bit unsure where to put these, but decided to put them here. One of the tools we have already discussed separately for a different reason: the 5 Whys. Another one we'll talk about later in the implementation tools section: the is–is not approach. I'm not going to dwell too much on the specific tools here, but more on the thinking behind the use of them. However, one of the most effective in root cause analysis is the Fishbone chart, named, not surprisingly, because it looks a little bit like a fish skeleton. Let's take a brief look at it and how it works in Figure 7.

The idea is that you state the problem and write it in the head of the fish. The main areas of the problem causes make up the big ribs, then possible causes associated with that area become small bones sprouting from the ribs; here the fish analogy starts to break down a bit, but the overall effect is OK. The important thing is that you capture as many possibilities as you can, so that you can either

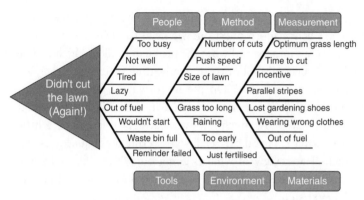

Figure 7   Example Fishbone Chart, aka Ishikawa Diagram

confirm or reject them based on the investigation. This really stops you jumping to conclusions and forces a rigorous investigation, as long as you do this part properly, that is! It does have limitations, like not showing the interrelations between causes, but is still very effective and, above all, simple, a characteristic that always appeals to me.

The process of root cause analysis

Now having mentioned a couple of tools, let's move on to the steps. Effective root cause analysis follows a very focused and disciplined thought process. Again, this is really quite obvious when you think about it; the steps in this process are:

- Define the problem.
- Get to the root cause.
- Solve the problem.
- Make sure the solution sticks.

Let's take a quick tour of each of these.

Define the problem   OK, this should be pretty straightforward, right? The engine's overheating. There, done that, on to the next stage. Not so fast, there's a bit more to do here before we move on, there are a few more questions we need to answer before we can really say we understand what the problem is, like: which engine? If we have a fleet, are all of them overheating or just one car? Where is it when it overheats? On the motorway, in the town, crossing the Sahara? When does it overheat? After a few hours, immediately, intermittently? How much is it overheating? Off the scale, a little bit above normal? As you can see, by answering these questions, we get a much clearer view of what is going on, which will make finding the cause a lot easier and stop us running down a lot of blind alleys in the next step.

Get to the root cause   Now for the really tough part, where we need to turn ourselves into robots and use those tools mentioned above as well as a few others like Pareto charts and correlation charts to get to the root cause. The specific tools to use will be defined by the particular situation, but the important thing is that you have to keep going and going until you can prove that every scrap of evidence is explained by the identified root cause. If anything does not fit, you're not done! Also bear in mind that there may be more than one root cause operating together, and this can make things really hard. One way to test if you have the root is to set up the same conditions and see if you can replicate the problem. Not always possible or desirable depending on the problem, but a useful way to test your theory. Once you have got to this point, you're in a very good place to define how you are going to monitor the effectiveness of the solution, so do this now while it's all fresh in your mind. It will pay dividends later in the "make it stick" stage.

Solve the problem   Not too much to say here unless I want to write another book on problem-solving techniques, but there are a few dos and don'ts. Don't jump on the first idea and run with it. Take some time to consider a few solution options; the not-so-obvious solution might actually be better. Do get a mix of people involved:

people who are living with the problem; outsiders who are not too close; the planet-sized-brain person; the artist who always seems to have the whacky ideas. All of these people will look at it from a different angle and between them come up with some really good solutions. Do make sure that you test that the solution is going to fix the problem properly and not generate another problem somewhere else. Look for ways the proposed solution might fail and understand the implications of these before implementing it using Failure Mode and Effect Analysis (FMEA). Do make sure that the solution you have arrived at doesn't just solve the current instance of the problem but prevents it happening again.

Once you have your solution, it needs to be implemented. This will also take planning and effort to do, so make sure that everyone is geared up to do what they need to do. Finally, write it all down and communicate what you have done. If people need to change what they do or how they behave, they need to know and understand why. This leads nicely to the final stage.

Making it stick   This is actually the hardest part of all. How many instances of "fixed today, broken again tomorrow" have you witnessed in life? Hundreds probably. This is because everyone went home after the party was over and forgot this last bit. Making it stick has two main parts that need to be in place to be successful.

Firstly the easy one, there needs to be some mechanism to monitor if the solution implemented is delivering the goods. Are we seeing a sustainable improvement? If not, then either the solution was not all it was cracked up to be, or the second part of "making it stick" has not been done.

Now the hard one, the hearts and minds. Most solutions to problems involve people doing something or reacting to something in a different way. For this to happen, the people involved need to understand what they need to do differently and why it is important that they do it, the "minds" part. This will require good communication and maybe some training, but this is only half the story, the other half is the "hearts" part: they have to believe in the solution and want to do things differently. This will take time, effort and good interpersonal skills to get people to this point.

If either of these aspects is not taken care of or fails, then the solution will not be sustainable.

Voice of the Customer

This might sound very simple, after all isn't it just asking the customer for their views? There is actually a lot more to it than that, and while you do need to ask the customer, figuring out what they mean and translating it into something you can act on is something else entirely.

Let's start by defining what we mean by Voice of the Customer, or VoC for short. VoC means that we translate everything we do into terms that express the value it brings to the customer. Let's take a very simple and everyday example: I need to buy some food. OK, first off, who is the customer? Let's say in this case it is my family. What is the VoC for my family in this case? Buying food is valuable for them in that I provide sustenance for my family, which keeps them healthy and allows them to be fed before they need to go out this evening. All sounds a bit crass, but let's look a little at what we've done here. We have now qualified the action, buying food, with the value it brings to the family: being adequately full, keeping them healthy while enabling them to do their evening activities. By specifying this, it puts some parameters around buying food, which were not there before. If I was just told to go and buy food, I might have bought some unhealthy junk food, not enough to feed the whole family and brought it back just when they needed to leave – failure on all counts!

So where do we get the information we need to be able to specify the VoC for our businesses? Well, we go ask them through as many means as possible: customer surveys, online shopping reviews, market research and, probably the most valuable, customer complaints.

These sources will provide a wealth of useful input from your customers to start interpreting into true VoC, but as the example above demonstrates, we are only at the start of the process. We need to convert these fairly fluffy statements into something we can take action on and measure if we are going to get better.

This part of the VoC process is called getting to the Critical to Customer Requirements or CCRs. This is the translation to something measurable. Let's take a real example which is used in the Six Sigma training involving lawn mower design requirements.

A lawn mower manufacturer received some feedback that its lawn mowers were difficult to start and were putting off potential customers. As a result, there was an improvement project kicked off to solve this problem. They could have just accepted the feedback, made some improvements and re-launched the mower onto the market only to find that the feedback was still not that good; better, but still not good enough to really improve sales. So they decided to employ VoC techniques to arrive at the CCRs that allowed them to specify clearly what improvements were needed to make the difference. The thought chain below shows the logic that was used to come to the right solution:

- The feedback says: "Your mowers are difficult to start."
- The requirement is: The mower must start quickly without discomfort to the operator.
- The CCRs are: The mower must start in no more than 2 pulls of no more than 600 mm with a pulling force of no more than 2.5 kg.

Now we have translated the customer view into some data to feed back to the design team to get it right. Getting these data will require a bit more than just scanning the available feedback and letters; it will mean getting out there, asking a few questions using some of the "5 Why" approach and then validating your answers back with the customer, but it will also mean that you are more likely to solve the problem. The actual result here was that the new design met all the CCRs, complaints stopped and sales started to grow.

The knock-on effect of this was that the marketing guys got hold of it and turned the now solved problem into competitive advantage by starting an advertising campaign with the slogan "Guaranteed to start by the first or second pull". Sales went through the roof and have stayed there! If you look around you can still see this slogan printed on the name plate of their mowers more than two decades after they solved the problem. Next time you go into a garden centre or DIY store have a look and see if you can spot it.

Does all this sound a bit familiar? It should do, the thought process is root cause analysis step one, define the problem, which we covered only a few moments ago. Adaptations of this approach are used to understand what needs to be done to improve the business results and to test if a customer-focused improvement initiative will actually benefit the business at the end of the day: this is called Voice of the Business, or VoB.

There are many, many more diagnostic tools available but I've picked out a few of the most useful and which apply to just about anything you care to consider.

Implementation tools

Now on to the tools that help us actually deliver and sustain the results we are looking for with the design, the implementation tools.

Standardisation

This topic covers quite a few subject areas and is very powerful. If you remember, earlier in the book we explained that variability is the death of Lean. Well, here we are going to discuss a few ways to take some of this variability out without having to do a load of analysis and redesign work. Just by applying some simple techniques and a bit of work, you can make a world of difference to both efficiency and quality. Again, many of these ideas apply to just about any situation.

Standard Work

The simple version of Standard Work is making sure things are done the same way, every time. You define one way of doing something, write it down, train everyone that needs to know how to do it in that one way, then make sure that it's being done the same way every time. Again, this all sounds very obvious, but in most places and situations, there will be little variations in the way different people do the same job. This can be the order in which they do things, the time they take to do it or the level of detail they go to. Just ask two people to empty the dishwasher and you'll see what I mean. Some will empty the top before the bottom, some will take four plates at a time to the cupboard, others will take two, and so on. None of these different ways of emptying the dishwasher are necessarily wrong, but they will end up with slightly different results: emptying the top first can result in drips on the things in the bottom; taking four plates instead of two is quicker, but may be more likely to chip the plates; and so on. As we've said many times before, eliminating these variations will lead to better quality and, through this, better total productivity, even if the way that's being used as the standard isn't the best way.

The more advanced version of Standard Work takes this a bit further and defines a theoretical best way by assuming everything works to the optimum. This is then used as the benchmark to drive improvement ideas to get there. After each improvement, the write down, train, manage process is repeated. Remember the Formula One tyre change story earlier in this book? This is an example of what I mean. But how do you go about arriving at this theoretical best?

The first thing to understand here is that there need to be limits on the expectations. If you can apply as much cash as you want coupled with intergalactic traveller technology and a good dose of magic, anything is possible. Not many of us have access to these types of resources, not usually even the money, so we have to be practical. This usually means that we start off with the assumption that we can't improve the underlying process, but we can organise around it better. Here's an example.

The process is attaching a hook to a string, the hook has a hollow end into which the end of the string is placed and the end of the hook is then pressed in a die to close the end of the hook onto the string securing to the hook. These assemblies are produced in batches of 500 at a time, after which the press has to be set up for making a different size. At the end of each batch a pull test is carried out on a sample of the batch to check that the hooks are properly attached, and then some paperwork is filled in.

To arrive at the theoretical best, we need to get a time for each of the different steps in the process. If any of you have done Time and Motion Studies, or were a rate fixer in the good (or bad?) old days of piece work, you'll know exactly what I'm on about here. In our example it works like this.

An average demonstrated time for each part of the process is calculated by timing the processes several times.

Getting ready:

- Fetching the next batch and reading the paperwork to find out the size.
- Resetting the press and checking that it is set correctly.
- Organising the strings and the hooks near to the press so that they can be worked on without leaving the press.
- Setting up the box for the finished assemblies.

Making the product:

- Picking up the hook and the string.
- Placing the end of the string into the hollow end of the hook.

- Placing the assembly onto the press die, pressing the foot pedal to operate the press and the cycle of the press.
- Picking up the now-joined assembly and putting in the box of finished assemblies.

Finishing the batch:

- Taking out five random samples from the finished assembly box.
- Taking the samples to the pull test machine (this is a short walk as it's shared equipment).
- Conducting the pull tests.
- Filling in the batch paperwork with the quantity produced, the pull test results and some other information.
- Taking the box of finished assemblies and the paperwork to the next process waiting area and returning to the press.

The average times for each of the steps in making the product are added together and the result multiplied by 500, as this is the nominal batch size. The average times for all the steps in getting ready and finishing the batch are added together and the total added to the making total. The result of all this is the Standard Work value for the job. Notice that we have included all the things that need to be done, including all the non-value-adding steps like walking to the pull tester.

So, how does this differ from what actually happens? Typically, you work out from the calculation above what should be made in a shift, and then look at the shift production records; you usually notice a big difference, sometimes up to 50%. This is due to all the distractions and problems that people encounter in a normal day which don't make it into the Standard Work calculations, these include: breakdowns; the string getting tangled occasionally; new staff who are still getting up to speed; failed pull tests which mean that the batch has to be reworked and other such problems.

By understanding the causes of the difference and eliminating them, very significant improvements in output can be made with very little investment. Very rarely is the only solution buying a new machine or asking people to work harder.

Another application of Standard Work that has been made very public has some very beneficial side effects. The designers of this process have used this as a marketing ploy to improve their image as well as make life easier for all of us. However, the real purpose was to reduce the effort needed to process the information and cut down on errors. The application is – tax returns.

Tax forms used to have a lot of free format space and what needed to be put into it was sometimes not at all clear. This meant that tax returns were often incomplete, or had errors which choked up the whole process with queries and rework both for you and the tax office. Now, however, the forms are simple, and follow a clear flow with many of the options being simply "yes" or "no", with clear directions on where to go next in both cases. This forces a standard way of filling them in and ensures that information is provided to the people processing them in a consistent way. Both these factors have greatly reduced the errors and confusion on both sides, making the whole process much less painful for all concerned, except for the tax bill you get. That's just as painful as it was before, if not more so!

Centre-lining

This is a fancy term for something I'm positive everyone has done many times without thinking. But when you apply it to complex equipment that needs a lot of setting up for different products, the benefits are huge. What centre-lining means is that you find the nominal settings for the equipment you are using for each of the major products you are making and either write down the settings or, better still, physically mark the positions on the equipment. This means that next time you come to make that product, all you need to do is line up the marks and you will be very close to where you need to be to start work almost immediately rather than having to spend hours setting up from scratch. All that needs to happen now is to make minor tweaks to take account of material or environmental changes.

There is a really good example of this that anyone who has played in a band using an amplifier will instantly recognise. If you haven't, then next time you go to a gig where you're close enough to the stage to see anything, have a quick peak at the lead guitarist's amplifier if you get a chance. I'll bet the controls are covered with sticky tape with little numbers or marks on. Anyone who plays electric guitar will tell you that it takes forever messing around with the EQ, gain, master volume, reverb and all the other stuff to get just the sound you are looking for. Once you've found it, you'll never find it again unless you record exactly where all the knobs and switches were at the time. When you're playing on stage, you don't have an hour between each song to reset all the knobs. By marking the positions on tape attached to the scale with the number of the song you are playing, you can change the sounds to what you want very quickly. That is centre-lining. Of course, the rock stars have tech guys setting up all the gear and swapping it out throughout the gig, but us mere mortals have to do it ourselves, so any help is welcome.

A more industrial application would be a printing press. If you've ever seen a four-colour reel-fed printing press, it's a mass of rollers, valves, tensioners and other stuff, all of which needs to be set exactly to get the right colour balance, alignment and intensity without smearing the ink or tearing the paper to shreds as it goes though at a million miles per hour. Setting all these up can take days for a complex job. Centre-lining can take several hours out of this setting up process for the same reasons above. It won't be absolutely spot on, but it will be close.

Also, each colour station is actually a separate machine with its own alignment adjustments. Over time, the individual colour stations can get progressively out of alignment with each other as the operator tweaks each one to get the finished product looking right, job after job. This misalignment is impossible to see just by looking at it, even with measuring equipment, but it has a big effect on the results, as you end up putting one colour station deliberately out of alignment to compensate for a misalignment in a previous colour station. The result is that when running, the entire press needs constant tweaking to get a consistent result rather than being set up, started and then left alone. The only way out of this situation when it's got too far out of whack is to completely tear apart the entire press, rebuild and calibrate to a fixed datum line. This is very rarely, if ever, done, as it is such a huge task and can take the press out of commission for weeks. Very often it needs an engineer from the original manufacturer to do it. So, in most cases they soldier on and continue to tweak away. It's for this reason that multicolour printing is seen as a black art, with skilled operators considered to be nothing less than magicians.

If the press had been centre-lined when it was installed, much of this problem could have been avoided. Each time the press is set up for a new job, the centre-lining will bring it back into factory state alignment each time. Less reliance on magicians and better, more reliable results!

"IS–IS NOT" thinking

The tool in this part is the "IS–IS NOT"; it would be better described as the "might be–is not" tool since only the "IS NOT" is really relevant until you get to the end. This is so simple it is often overlooked but is very, very powerful if used ruthlessly. This is all about the process of elimination and, to quote a very famous fictional detective, "Once you eliminate the impossible, whatever remains, no matter how improbable, must be the truth." To illustrate this, let's look at a real example that had the engineers and chemists in a chemical production plant baffled for months until someone used this process to eliminate the "IS NOTs".

A chemical process taking place in a reaction vessel in the main reactor hall was, in most cases, very reliable, giving high yields and a stable outcome. However, over the past 18 months, it would occasionally all go wrong and the batch had to be rejected. It was one of those nagging intermittent problems that hit you just when you thought the problem had gone away all by itself, although they rarely do. The process needed a slightly elevated temperature to work but was highly sensitive to being at the right temperature. There was a small heater with a quite sophisticated temperature monitoring and control system. The chemical process itself generated a bit of heat, but not enough to get the mixture to the right temperature. In each failure case, there was a small temperature spike recorded which lasted for about 30 minutes of the five-hour process which was identified as the culprit. The hard part was to track down what was causing it. All kinds of theories were postulated and tested and all came up with nothing. This went on for about two years before someone, completely unconnected with the problem and who was not an engineer or a chemist, used the "IS–IS NOT" approach to the problem, much to the initial chagrin of the engineer and chemists who had been working on this the whole time, as it seemed a bit of a simplistic approach to them after all the science that had been employed to date.

Anyway, our friend started asking a series of binary questions that could only be answered with "yes" or "no", such as: "Does the spike occur at the same time in the process each time?" – No. "Is the spike the same length each time" – Yes. "Is the spike the same height each time? – No, and so on. After a while, they managed to eliminate the heater element, the mixer and the heater controller, as eventually they ended up in the "IS NOT" column. After a few more, they managed to come to the conclusion that the problem was not with the process at all, but was environmental. This was a major breakthrough and a big relief as well, but they still hadn't pinpointed the problem, so off we go again. "Is the ambient temperature in the reactor hall too high or fluctuating when the spike happens?" – No. "Does the problem seem to occur at the same time of day?" – Yes, but not exactly – ah, a clue! The next part of the investigation looked at the frequency of the problem, which showed that it only happened in the months of May and June, but not every day. By this time there was a feeling that they were close to a solution.

What could possibly cause the temperature of the reaction vessel to increase in only two months of the year, at a particular time of day, when the rest of the reactor hall remained at the same temperature? To find out they put a simple temperature sensor next to the vessel and waited for a spike to happen. Sure enough, early in May there was a spike and the alarm bells went off. Everyone rushed to the scene to finally find out what was happening and put the problem to bed. There, in all its glory was the reaction vessel illuminated like some signal from the gods by a beautiful shaft of sunlight. Everyone looked up and saw the problem instantly. The roof of the hall was glass, but had been painted on the inside with reflective paint to keep the sun out and stop the temperature rising. Three and a half years ago, one of the panes had cracked and was replaced, but whoever replaced it forgot to paint it. In the months of May and June, if the sun was shining at a particular time of day, the sun came through the gap to shine on the reaction vessel, causing it to heat up just enough to spoil the batch. After thirty minutes, the sun had moved, the vessel was in shade again and the temperature returned to normal, but the damage had already been done. A five-minute job with some left over paint solved the problem for good, after two years of investigation which had got them nowhere. Such is the power of "IS–IS NOT". This is a true story!

Good day vs. bad day

You won't find this one in any of the books, which surprises me because, just like of lot of the best tools, it is very simple. It's so simple and uses the same principles and techniques that are all over any case study or book on Lean, Six Sigma or Failure Mode Analysis, and so on, that there is no need to bang on at length about it here.

Essentially what you are doing is turning problem solving and root cause analysis on its head. If you look at virtually any improvement project, what you will find is a huge amount of effort expended on trying to find the causes for failure, then thinking of ways to prevent them. What good day vs. bad day does is acknowledge that although sometimes things go badly, you should also recognise that there are usually an equal number of days when the stars align and everything works. You know what I mean, the days when you get 50% higher output and no defects for no apparent reason; these are the good days. Very often when this happens, everyone wipes the sweat off their brow and puts it all down to good fortune shining on them that day, while at the same time still trying to figure out why yesterday had been such a mess. But let's think about this phenomenon a bit. Things going well are not due to divine intervention, luck or magic; it's due to all the variables of the process behaving themselves at once. So, rather than spending all your time trying to solve what went wrong on the bad day, why not spend as much time trying to pinpoint why everything went right on the good day? If we can figure this out, and replicate it, we'd have a whole lot more good days, which would make a big difference to the overall performance. This is the essence of this technique.

The starting point for this is to have some solid data about what was going on for a few bad days and a few good days, which means that someone has to be there watching and recording what's happening. Once you have a fairly reliable set of data, you then start the detailed investigation, not into what went wrong on the bad day, but what the differences were between the good and the bad. This is usually quite a bit easier to do, as you have two reference points to compare. By doing this, you can quite quickly identify the controlling variables which make the difference out of the plethora of things going on and work on replicating the conditions which made these all pull in the right direction. All the tools you would normally use in root cause analysis work just as well here, so there's nothing new to learn, you are just applying them to a different situation.

I've used this approach very often to great effect over the years at varying degrees of detail, from the very formal Six Sigma DMAIC approach to simply going and asking someone who has just recorded a best ever day: "So what happened? Why did it all go right?" Very often, just by asking you will get enough to make a few changes and make a measurable long-term difference.

Kaizen Events

Let's face it, no one can write a book on Lean without giving Kaizen a mention. After all, it is one of the primary vehicles of Lean: engagement-driven continuous improvement; the place all the other tools come out to play. So, not to be the only book to ignore this, here we go, a section on Kaizen.

Kaizen is a Japanese phrase from two words: 改 善, Kai and Zen. There are a number of literal translations as it doesn't directly translate to English well, but the common ones are: improve, change for better, and the longer one, take apart and put back better. Whatever you choose to let it mean for you, the message is the same. What we are going to look at here is a brief overview of what a Kaizen Event is and how they fit into the broader scheme of things.

The anatomy of a Kaizen Event

The two keys to a successful Kaizen Event are:

- Selecting the right subject area for the event.
- Thorough planning.

Let's look at the subject area first. On the face of it, this should be fairly simple, right? We have our high-level current state VSM all duly marked up with a host of potential improvement areas. All we need to do is pick one of these at random and we should be fine. Well, in theory yes, but, as usual, things aren't quite that simple. There are a couple of criteria that need to be satisfied when selecting a target area: the event shouldn't be more than a week in duration, and as a result of the week's effort, there must have been a visible change. That doesn't mean that everything needs to be completed and working; it's OK to have some outstanding implementation actions or follow-ups, but the team must feel that they have achieved something concrete. Now when you look over the opportunities on the VSM, this will probably discount a significant bunch of them, but hopefully there will be enough left to allow you some choice for a few Kaizen Events. The current state VSM is not the only idea source for Kaizen Events and you don't want to stifle the enthusiasm you have worked so hard to generate; look to suggestions from people doing the work as well.

That takes care of the selection, so what about the planning? Not quite so fast, we haven't finished with the selection just yet. A Kaizen Event will bring together a number of people with different skills and experience and these people will need to be in the same place for most of the week working together to identify a solution, design it and implement it. Therefore, it makes sense to pick something that is fairly local and can be tackled by a local team. This isn't a rule, there may be a need to draught in people from other locations for certain skills, but it helps. It also helps with the motivational aspect of Kaizen, as the people making the changes are going to be living and benefiting from the fruits of their labours afterwards. So, does that now take care of the selection, can we move on to the planning? Yes we can.

Even if we had the best subject area for an event, but just threw six to eight people in a room with a "go fix that" instruction and left them to it for a week, it is unlikely that they would be very successful. Oh, they may well come up with some ideas and actually deliver something, but the outcome would probably be nowhere near as good as it could have been with a bit of good planning and preparation up front. To help understand this better let's take a look at what a typical five-day, or one-week event schedule of activities looks like.

Day 1:

- Introductions – Make sure everybody knows everyone else and what they are bringing to the party. Go through how the event is expected to play out.

- Set objectives – Understand the purpose of the event subject area and the expectations for the scope of the changes and levels of improvement.
- Tools familiarisation – Make sure everyone is up to speed on what tools are likely to be used and how to use them; this isn't full-on training, but enough of a refresher to get everyone on the same page.
- Agree roles and responsibilities – There are numerous tasks to do and roles to fulfil. The team needs to discuss and agree who is going to do what and play what roles, that includes someone to act as the event leader!
- Data familiarisation – There will have been a significant amount of data collected about the event subject area, (hopefully in advance!); this needs to be sifted through and understood by the team and any anomalies or inconsistencies sorted out.
- Get ready for the first real work session – This means setting up the "war room" as the team wants it, lining the walls with brown paper and dishing out all the pencils and sticky notes.

All of this usually takes up the entire first day. If you can get through it quicker, great, but don't rush into the next lot of activities at the expense of doing a good job on the above.

Day 2:

- Detailed current state value stream mapping – This looks only at the subject area for the event rather than the end-to-end one done previously, and is at a much more detailed level. In this one all the data boxes need to be filled in!
- Specific improvement brainstorming – Getting all the creative stuff on the wall!
- New process design and future state VSM creation – Organising the above ideas and building them into a new way of working,

then documenting it on the wall. Hence the acres of brown paper you applied to the walls the previous day.

- New roles and responsibilities definition – Understanding what the new process will do to roles, responsibilities and resources, again documented as above.
- Plan for the next three days – Creating an activity plan for all the implementation work to be done: what and by whom.

This is a big day and at this point everyone will be very relieved that they did not bite off more than they could chew as the scope for the event. You will now have the blueprint for what you are going to implement over the next three days.

Day 3:
You thought Day 2 was busy? Now the real work starts and the pace hots up even more. The team, and all the other people the team needs to tap into, get to work on all the immediate change actions and solve problems as they arise, as there will be many cases of "oops!" or "didn't see that one coming" or "does anyone have a plan B?" Mission Control keeps tabs on what's happening and oils the wheels where necessary to keep the momentum up.

At the end of Day 3, if things have gone reasonably well, there will be a great deal accomplished, with real changes having happened. Even at this stage, people in the workplace will have noticed that things aren't quite the same.

The final act of Day 3 is a short post mortem of the day, a re-jig of the plan, if necessary, and a pep talk to keep the enthusiasm up ready for Day 4.

Day 4:
Day 4 is a continuation of Day 3 where many of the activities started are completed and training on the new ways is done to help embed the changes.

It's at the end of this day that you really find out if you've bitten off more than you could chew with the scope you agreed on

Day 1. Hopefully, with some realistic ambitions and some on-the-fly changes made during the previous days, the team will collapse in the team room at the end of the day and feel good about all they have done, while mopping copious amounts of sweat from their brows.

This day marks the end of the immediate changes, but the event doesn't stop here.

Day 5:

Doing all the hard work above is great and will make a difference to a lot of people, not just those involved in the event. However, there is a need to shout about it and feed back to the leadership a few things.

Firstly, celebrate and brag about all that's been achieved. This is very important, particularly if this is the first Kaizen Event being staged in the business. In many cases, leadership is really not aware of what to expect or how much can get done when the focus is there. This is the opportunity to do a bit of education on that.

Secondly, change does not happen overnight and many of the things achieved will need to be underpinned by good management and leadership while they become embedded. Also, things like KPIs and metrics might need to be changed. This is the role of the leaders and they need to be told what exactly they need to do going forward if all the hard work is going to be for the long-term good.

Finally, not everything will be completed and there will be some mid- to longer-term changes that need to happen, things which take longer than the week of the event. All these need to be clearly documented, a commitment made to do them and people put on the spot to deliver them.

All of the above happens as part of the report back prepared and presented on Day 5.

So, that's it. The event has been a rip-roaring success and we can all have a beer and go home happy. Not quite, remember the term "continuous improvement"? Well, this means that these events are not just a one-off. There needs to be a review fixed for some point in the future to do two things: check that the expected improvements in performance have happened and are sustained; and come back and do the whole thing over again to deliver the next raft of improvements.

Now you can all go and get a beer.

If you don't have rhythm, you can't dance!

I'll warn you in advance, this section is quite long compared to the others in this chapter. That's because this is a very powerful tool that has proved itself extremely valuable over and over again but is very often misunderstood. It's out here on its own because it spans both categories of tools: diagnostic and implementation.

The title of this section could have been "How to level load your production lines when you have a lot of products and demand is highly variable", but that's a bit of a mouthful and besides, I like the title I have better. Hundreds of finished products all with demand all over the place is the bane of most production managers' lives. When you're getting nice steady orders, life is simple: set up a line, match capacity to demand and off you go. But when everyone wants different amounts of different products, well, life just gets hard.

Enter rhythm! This is a really simple inventory planning and scheduling approach, which allows the right amounts of the right products to be produced on demand while level loading the plant and minimising working capital. In fact, it is so simple and so effective, most just don't believe it will work. I've had plenty of battles on this one! To anyone who has worked in the planning and scheduling world for some time, the idea of rhythm is a bit counter-intuitive. When you start to explain it, you get some very weird looks and "that can't work" comments. However, if you can persuade the powers that be to give it a try, the light bulbs go on very quickly once people see it working, then there's no going back.

Rhythm has its roots in the original Lean Planning Wheel concepts for minimising changeover downtime. The problem with planning wheels is that as soon as the demand for each product begins to fluctuate, everything starts to fall apart. This is because planning wheels fix the sequence and the timing, and as every maths student will tell you, in a three-variable equation, if you fix two, you automatically fix the third, which in this case is the quantity. Rhythm, however, takes the planning wheel approach a bit further by allowing the timing to flex. This then frees up the third variable and allows batch sizes and, hence, production frequencies to flex too while the sequence remains fixed. As I said, simple, but for someone steeped in master scheduling and planning wheels it can be a bit hard at first to reset the grey cells.

How it works

The rhythm concept comprises four main processes: three as part of the periodic supply planning process and one as part of the production execution process.

Planning

The first part of this is the inventory replenishment or buffer level calculation and, as mentioned in a previous chapter, this is the level to which inventory should be replenished by Production. The calculation is similar to a conventional strategic inventory buffer calculation. However, lead time is replaced by rhythm time (to be discussed later). Just like any other buffer, it can be forward-looking to provide a required inventory profile to cater for seasonality and demand trends, or based on historic demand patterns, or a combination of the two.

The next part is the rhythm calculation. Rhythm has three primary design parameters: sequence, rhythm time and minimum make quantity. Products are grouped by like production process and allocated to a production line based on this. All products falling into the process family should be included, irrespective of demand profile or if they are make to stock or make to order.

Production sequence for the line is determined by applying a changeover hierarchy to minimise the changeover downtime between one product and the next in the sequence. The most critical design parameter for rhythm is the rhythm time, which is the time expected to complete one full cycle of the rhythm sequence based on expected run time for the average demand for all the products on the wheel and the expected time for changeovers and the capacity of the line. A design rhythm time should be no more than one week if the full benefits of rhythm are to be realised; this, of course, means that aggressively reducing changeover time has to be a high priority.

All this changeover hierarchy talk sounds a bit complicated and indeed there are two ways to do it. To be pure about it, you need to clearly understand what is driving the differences in changeover time, usually there are about four or five key ones. Then you need to look at each changeover driver and analyse the time and the effort it takes to do each one. From that, develop a changeover matrix with columns ordered by changeover driver and sequence each product row of each column in descending time order, blah, blah, blah. The result of all this will be the optimal sequence. Simple, yes? Hmm … well, there is an easier way. A way I have used many times very successfully. Here's how it works – ready?

You get out of your seat, walk to the shop floor with your list of products in your hand, go up to one of the more experienced people working on the line you're trying to sequence and say: "Excuse me, if you had to make these (showing him or her the list) on that (pointing to the machine) what order would you do them in?" Ninety nine times out of a hundred, you will get your optimal sequence in five minutes and usually get a more accurate result!

The final part we need is the average demand for the total list of products. All we need to do here is work out the average demand over the rhythm time, in this case one week, for each SKU, then add them all together. Finally, add in the expected changeover times for a week by applying a minimum make quantity to the average demand. Using these parameters, we should plan to load the line to a minimum of 85% of total available capacity based on design rhythm time and average aggregate demand for the products on that line. The unallocated 15% of capacity is to provide for maintenance and other planned or unplanned downtime. A further enhancement is to factor in product value, so that high-value or high-margin products are triggered for production more frequently. If there's not enough capacity to make all the products on the list, some will have to be allocated to another line, which will have its own rhythm wheel.

Execution

Just as we talked about in the Planning and Scheduling section of Chapter 4, all we have done so far is set up rules. We haven't actually made anything yet. When we need to make something, there are three things we need to know: what to make, this is fixed by the sequence and if there is demand for it; when to make it, that's simple, when you've finished the previous one; and how much to make. OK, this is what we need to talk about. The first thing to understand about rhythm execution is that there is no fixed forward schedule or firm planning horizon. In theory, the quantity of the next product to be made can be determined at the time the previous product run has finished. However, in practice it's not quite that simple as at least some forward view is needed to get things ready. Typically, a report is run at the start of each shift, which gives a forward view of what is likely to be made in the next shift. This firm horizon is governed only by the length of time needed to stage and prepare materials for production.

The report, printed or displayed, is in rhythm sequence order and uses the following logic: for each product, current available inventory, in-transits and any open production orders are netted off against the buffer target. The result of this is compared to the minimum make quantity and, if greater, a production order is created for that amount (this can be modified to suit raw material batch sizes or packaging multiples if necessary). If the result is smaller, then the product is skipped and the next product in the sequence is reviewed in the same way. For MTO products, the requirement is simply the order quantity with no modification. A final check is made on material availability immediately prior to production and the production order is released and started. All of this happens a maximum of 24 hours before physical production of that product is started. Ideally, this could be within minutes of starting, but this is often not practical. At the start of the next shift or day, the current report is destroyed and a new one created to manage the next period of production. The traditional weekly schedule, which absorbs so much time being created, changed and changed again, can be dispensed with, freeing up time to manage events better. This last statement is very often the biggest barrier to rhythm. It is very hard for people to let go of their forward view of the world and trust that there will be something to do tomorrow, but you just don't know exactly what it is yet. They want that comfort blanket of the one-week or two-week schedule to look at, even though in their hearts they know it's all lies a day or two out.

Once one rhythm cycle is completed, the next starts immediately, whether the design rhythm time has expired or not. The result: in cycles where there is less than average aggregate demand, the rhythm cycle finishes early and the next is started; in cycles where there is greater than average aggregate demand, the rhythm cycle finishes late. This "breathing" of the rhythm to demand allows production to be continuous and level loaded at the line's design capacity, while output of individual products is in line with demand irrespective of the variability of the demand. With sufficient products in the sequence, the demand variability of individual products can be very large, but the aggregate variability will be within acceptable limits of +/– 20% of average in any one cycle.

"Hang on though, I don't want to be making all my products every week!" I hear you say. The answer is, you won't, a one-week rhythm time does not mean that every product is made every week; it means that every product has the opportunity to be made every week if there is demand for it.

The actual production frequency for any product is governed by the actual demand and the "minimum make quantity", the minimum practical and financial quantity of product that should be made on the line.

All of this means that in practice only about 30% of products on the rhythm wheel will trigger in any one week, but that will be a different 30% each time. Sure, some of the very high volume products will trigger every week. The more products on the wheel the better the process works, as the aggregate demand across them all becomes smoother and the size of rhythm time "breathing" becomes less.

Rhythm is applicable to almost any product demand profile; it is not restricted to products with stable demand with low week-to-week volatility. Rhythm is self-regulating and will recover from most demand and supply events without intervention. In addition, if a product's demand profile changes (say, an increasing demand trend over time), the make quantity calculation result will exceed the minimum make quantity more frequently and trigger production more frequently as a result.

This simple adaptation of a well-known approach also allows the traditional ABC analysis by volume or demand volatility, resulting in a predetermined production frequency for each segment, for example, daily, weekly, monthly, and so on, to be abandoned. The usual problem with ABC is that, as demand patterns change over time, no one bothers to update the ABC classification until things are very obviously out of whack and something goes wrong. With rhythm, if the demand goes up, the frequency of manufacture goes up too because it is controlled by the minimum make quantity. No one needs to do anything, it just happens on its own. All this results in a supply process that is simple, consistent and able to respond automatically to demand changes. This is one of the major departures from the well-known Planning Wheel logic.

While rhythm is best suited to a make-to-stock or VMI environment where there is visibility and management of inventory at the customer level, it is not restricted to this, rhythm can also work well in a pure make-to-order environment.

This all sounds too good to be true, everything runs on automatic; we all might as well just go home. Well, it's not quite that automatic, there is a need to keep a watchful eye on a few early warning indicators that things have changed so much that a redesign is needed. The primary early warning indicator for rhythm is "rhythm time attainment". This monitors the actual rhythm time for each cycle and provides early warnings of changes in either overall product demand for the line or changes in capacity. This should be monitored using a control chart with the upper and lower process control limits set by the rhythm design parameters. Any trends identified which violate these control limits indicate that something has changed and action may be necessary to resolve it – either fixing a problem or refreshing the rhythm design. Rhythm time trending low means smaller batches and wasted capacity on excessive changeovers; rhythm time trending high means that there will be more days of demand on the next cycle, which will further increase actual rhythm time and ultimately lead to service issues.

The final key component of rhythm that overarches all the others is discipline. Rhythm is a simple process with a few basic rules that can transform the efficiency and effectiveness of a supply chain. However, all will be lost if the organisation does not understand the rules and does not have the discipline and leadership to stick to them when the going gets tough. This last point is the reason behind choosing a short rhythm time: it's much easier to get people to stick to the sequence and not push in that "urgent" order if there is only a few days to when its turn comes round in the sequence. If this were a month, the discipline wouldn't last one cycle before someone senior was screaming "Foul".

In conclusion

We've talked about a number of tools in this chapter, but in reality we have only scratched the surface of what there is available in the Lean toolbox. In the glossary there are references to some more that you might want to find out more about, but could not be given an airing here.

However, the tools above are some of the most useful and if applied properly should be able to get you started and, at least, make you aware of where some of the other tools might be applied.

I can't really overemphasise the importance of value stream mapping. It is the starting point of the process and helps to guide you through what needs to change and what that change should be. In whatever form you use it, as a thumbnail for understanding or a rigorous analysis tool, its value is almost boundless.

12

A FEW WORDS ON TECHNOLOGY

A few words on technology? Ha! That's not going to be easy. You could fill a whole book on this subject, but I'll give it a try.

There's no getting away from it, we live in an IT world now – virtually every business has some form of IT-based system to manage just about everything. In today's complex global environment, it's almost a requirement to have this just to be able to comply with ever-stricter financial rules and regulations.

As a result, the ubiquitous Enterprise Requirements Planning system (ERP) is a fact of life and can't be ignored.

For a lot of what ERP systems do, this is all fine and dandy and there are no conflicts with the Lean world. However, where Lean and ERP cross swords is in the world of production planning and scheduling; here they are coming at it from totally opposite directions. I'm not going to give chapter and verse on this as I've already covered the difference between forecast-push and demand-driven approaches to supply in a previous chapter, but what you do need to know is that virtually all ERP systems have a forecast-push MRP engine sitting pretty right at the heart of them. And herein lies the problem. This means that they are not capable of properly supporting a Lean environment, as the underlying assumptions and planning rules are just not compatible with a Lean, demand-driven world.

This understanding is what I'm going to attempt to provide an introduction to here. I should add a health warning to this though.

I'm only going to scratch the surface here and the devil is in the detail. Understanding exactly how your ERP has been configured and the implications of switching parts of it off on the operation of the rest of the business is a minefield, and will need a lot of work and input from specialists both inside and outside to understand and get right.

The only other option is to leave well alone and manage the local operation using spreadsheets and other visual tools, then replicate the outcomes in the ERP systems with manual entry. Unfortunately, this had been the only option until recently, which tells us why end-to-end Lean demand-driven supply has been slow to take hold across the board. Running a large business on the back of spreadsheets is not a scalable or sustainable solution. As an interesting footnote here, a recent survey showed that 80% of all larger businesses which have an ERP system implemented rely on spreadsheets for a significant amount of their tactical operation. Makes you think, doesn't it?

Now let's get stuck into the topic!

What's good, what's not

Now let me make it clear, I'm not here to bash the ERP providers, but from a Lean perspective there are a few things which really are a bit clunky to say the least. However, let's start with what an ERP system is good for.

This is actually quite easy. If you want a clear view of the current status of the universe as we know it, and want to drill down into almost infinite levels of detail, then you have the right tool. In terms of areas of the business this covers, that list is quite extensive too:

- Master data on just about anything from products and services to customers to suppliers to people in your organisation.
- Tracking and reporting on any transaction you can name; for example, stock movements, production status, goods receipts, sales and shipments, cash in and cash out to name but a few.

- Medium to long-term planning of capacity, demand and production.
- Batch traceability and order or account tracking.
- Financial management, budgeting and tracking.
- Reports, reports and more reports until you've pulped every tree on the planet!

As you can see from this, there's a lot these monsters can do, covering a wide range of business areas. "So what's the problem?" I hear you ask. Well, as alluded to before, the problem is with deciding exactly what to do right here right now to meet the customer needs. In other words, execution. So let's create a similar list for the not-so-good stuff, shall we?

- Telling your workforce or supplier what to do or deliver to the customer today, and the next few days, which is in line with the customer needs.
- Providing a clear and stable view of what is needed in the short term, in other words, the next few days to satisfy the same goal.

OK, this list is quite short, but it's really critical. If you can't get a clear and stable view of this, then you're going to end up making the wrong thing and paying for it in customer service problems, high inventory or running around like there's no tomorrow trying to rectify the situation before you get stung. In reality, you'll probably end up suffering in all these areas.

Closing the gaps

Now we've understood what is OK and not-so-OK about our ERP system when it comes to supporting Lean, let's look at what parts we need to bypass or change to make it work better. Before we do this, it's important to understand a little more about the real differences in philosophy when it comes to ERP planning functionality and Lean ways of working. The following table attempts to clarify this to some extent:

Traditional ERP Approach		Lean-enabled ERP
Uses forecast and EBQs to drive production planning and quantities.	→	Uses actual customer demand to drive production quantities based on replenishment to target inventory buffer levels or fulfilment of make-to-order items.
Uses forecast, EBQs and process reliability to determine safety stocks.	→	Uses historical demand, known events, the forecast and process reliability to determine strategic buffer targets and size inter-process kanbans.
Uses finite scheduling at each work centre to determine production timing, requires judgement and multiple intervention on a day-to-day basis.	→	Uses optimal production sequencing or "rhythm" at one work centre only to replace scheduling decisions. Signals transmitted to other work centres through kanbans or other flow mechanisms.
Uses rough cut capacity planning and finite scheduling to determine a feasible schedule.	→	Uses rough cut capacity planning against historical demand, forecast and future known "Events" to plan medium and longer-term capacity requirements. Buffers allow for short-term balancing and scheduling to be managed locally.
Uses MRP to plan weekly production of finished and component parts.	→	Uses MRP to support longer-term planning and supplier relationships.

Uses transactional data to track progress and provide input to next scheduling run.	→	Manages flow through kanbans and FIFO rules, transactional data only collected for compliance, quality, financial purposes and to record arrival at the next buffer.
Uses advanced planning tools to provide visibility along the extended value chain and manage day-to-day execution.	→	Uses advanced planning tools to provide visibility along the extended value chain to provide "what if" capability and assist with "Event" planning and management.

What this means is that there are some parts of your ERP systems that have just become redundant, at least for planning and scheduling purposes, so really, these could be switched off or not implemented in the first place:

- MRP is not needed for creating planned orders for production and purchasing.
- The finite scheduling function is not needed, replaced by "work-to" lists or "rhythm" and buffer triggers.
- Availability checking and most Available to Promise (ATP) functions are not needed. Buffer status and known demand make the need unnecessary.

All of this, when coupled with visual controls for in-process tracking and reduced lead times, means that the need to record every movement through the factory in the ERP system becomes less important, resulting in reduced transactional data collection, storage, analysis and reporting needs of up to 75%.

Of course, this is all well and good, but if you don't replace these parts with something that will close the data loop, it'll all come crashing down around your ears. If this happens, I can assure you that it will be very visible in very high places and you will not be the most popular person in the world!

While the ins and outs of a modern, integrated ERP system are wildly complex, the changes aren't really that complicated to provide a minimum demand-driven solution. In fact, there are only three fundamental requirements:

- Stop MRP creating and changing orders in its relentless mission to preserve safety stock at all points in the supply chain as demand changes.
- Provide a mechanism to create a replenishment order when a buffer status drops below target by the minimum order quantity.
- Reconnect the loop with the ERP system so that the rest of the transaction path, all the way to the financials, is left intact and functioning.

The first of these requirements might seem like just switching off MRP. Indeed, this will work, but remember, MRP is actually quite useful for loading and capacity planning and long lead time materials requirements visibility, so we don't actually want to just switch it off. What we need to do is find a way of disconnecting the planning part of MRP from the execution part. Actually, it is OK to continue letting planned orders be created – the planning part – as long as they are not released – the execution part – since, in our new world, they are for reference only and any changes can be ignored. Therefore, the part you need to switch off is automatic and manual release or firming of planned orders generated by MRP. This will include production orders, purchase orders or stock transfer orders, depending on how you have set up your system and the extent to which you are implementing demand-driven supply. This clears the path for the next requirement, which is to generate demand-driven orders.

Now this is where it all gets a bit tricky, and many have resorted to spreadsheets to do this. However, the easiest way to do this is by writing a report and adding it as a menu item on the planning and scheduling screen. Whatever option you choose, the requirements are the same, so let's look at what needs to be done. Each time a new production schedule or purchasing requirements list is needed, usually daily, the current inventory status needs to be exported from the ERP system in terms of on-hand inventory and current open orders. This needs to be compared with the buffer target and if the difference is greater than the minimum order quantity a new order needs to be created. This can be as simple as a list of order suggestions giving the part number, quantity needed and the location being replenished. This then acts as the new schedule or purchase order request list, which can be picked up and acted on by Production, Logistics or Purchasing dependent on the type of order. This list can also provide the raw requirements for rhythm should you need it, so it all fits together quite nicely. What all this means, of course, is that each time you need to have a fresh requirements list, there need to be data extracted from the ERP system which contains the current inventory and open order data. Now for the loop-closing part.

Closing the loop means kidding the ERP system that it has created all the needed orders by inputting the orders generated by the step above. If this is only a few orders in a fairly small company, this could simply involve manual creation and release of the orders on the list and the job is done. The ERP system then picks these up and carries on where it left off, faithfully tracking them through completion steps all the way to the financial records. In addition, this ensures that the right data are present in terms of open orders for the process cycle to start again from the top. For larger, more complex situations, a more automated approach will be needed, which imports the orders as a file transfer on a daily or more frequent basis.

So, from an execution perspective, that's about it. However, we haven't covered the planning part yet, which is setting the buffer targets in the first place. Again, your common or garden variety of ERP system doesn't do this too well, as they are usually set up for safety stock calculations. Again, this usually ends up being done externally. For each part, historical demand needs to be looked at and maybe some forecast data to give average volumes and to calculate demand variability. Other data needed include lead times, minimum order quantities and supply variability. All of this needs to be exported into a buffer calculator, which applies the buffer algorithms and comes up with a target inventory level for each part at each buffer location. This is then imported back into the ERP system to be used for step 2 above. If all this verbal gobbledegook leaves you a bit cold and wondering what all this really means, let me try to put it in a picture. Figure 8 shows where the interaction points are between a Lean demand-driven solution and one of the better-known ERP systems. Very simplified, but I hope it helps a little!

The good news is that there are now a couple of ERP bolt-on solutions that do support Lean and with the right integration with the backbone ERP system will work very well. However, you need to understand what system supports what process and how they will connect together to ensure that the whole remains complete, compliant and robust.

In conclusion

As I said at the start of this chapter, a few words, and indeed it only is a few, but I hope that these few words have given you some insight into what to do to ensure that you can support the new ways of working that Lean demands, as you go forward.

I've tried not to paint the ERP and MRP systems as villains in the show because they are not. Any medium to large company worth its salt needs a tool like this to keep track of what it's doing and committing to if it's going to survive in the modern world. It's just that for the critical few things needed in the Lean world, there is a bit of a mismatch that you will need to take into account and do something about. In my experience, it's not the tool that's the real problem here, it's the way it's implemented and by whom. The help you tend to get to implement ERP is very often myopic on anything but the way the system works; it's the system way or no way. I could wax lyrical on a past experience where a very well-known multinational company was well down the road of a very successful Lean journey, just to get it trampled over and killed by a

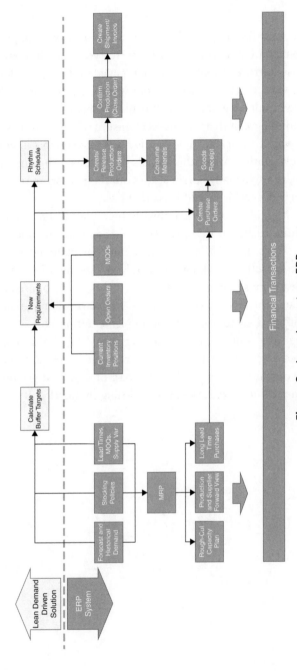

Figure 8 Lean Impact on ERP

corporate-wide ERP implementation because the people supporting the implementation just didn't get Lean. Ten years on, the company is only just starting to realise what happened and is now asking if there is a way to get back to the "old ways of Lean before ERP". Well there is, but it's going to be difficult for them.

The moral here, if there is one, is to ensure that the business dictates the ways of working and what is needed to support it, not the technology solution. While this sounds so obvious it shouldn't need saying, there are so many horror stories out there where the opposite has happened, I feel it should be said anyway.

One last point before I leave this chapter. I left a clue about this point a little earlier in this chapter: " ... redundant or not implemented ... " It's the "not implemented" bit. The planning, scheduling and transaction tracking parts of your average ERP systems tend to be the most complex and the most heavily customised parts. As you can probably guess, as soon as you start talking about the complexity and customisation, the implementation cost and time go through the roof. So, if you can get your Lean ways of working defined and in place before you commit to your ERP solution designs, you can save yourself a boatload of cash and get up and running a year or more earlier. Just a closing thought!

13

GETTING HELP

There were two phrases that sprung immediately into my head when I started to write this chapter:

"We are not alone"

and

"Don't try this at home!"

I think both of these have relevance in the context of implementing Lean in any situation, although the second one does sound like a bit of a plug for my chosen profession!

So, what do I mean here? Let's take a look, starting with the first one.

We are not alone

Lean has been around for a long time and no matter how long you've been at it, from just starting out to a battle-scarred Lean warrior, there are always going to be people out there who have been at it longer than you or have learned how to deal with that thorny issue you just can't seem to get your head around. And you know what? Most of them are quite happy to talk to you about it and give you the benefit of their wisdom. The following few paragraphs provide a peek into the most common ways of doing this, but there will be other ways too.

Partnering with other companies

I've seen this happen and be very successful many times. Indeed, when I was in industry, the company I worked for did just this to help accelerate the programme. This can vary in style from a casual relationship involving some visits to one another's sites with a tour and some workshops, to a more formal arrangement resulting in the development of a long-term relationship. This can be with one or more companies collaborating, sharing and learning as they progress on their Lean journey.

In the case I mentioned above, it was the latter. To my knowledge the relationship is still going on after several years and both parties are gaining a great deal of insight and support from each other. There have been exchange assignments where experienced Lean practitioners have been seconded for up to a year to the other company to provide insight and guidance on specific projects, or the programme as a whole. This type of relationship takes more effort to set up and administer than the more casual approach, but the mutual rewards can be very significant. Selecting the right partner is absolutely critical here. A lot of time, effort and expense can be wasted if there is not a good fit for both companies. To try to avoid this, here are a few suggestions of questions to consider:

- Where are they on their journey? If one party is just starting out and the other is a well-seasoned Lean organisation, then there will be a mismatch of benefit, with all the goodies going to the newbies. If the other guys are very philanthropic, then this might work, but it's unlikely. On the other hand, if both parties are at the same place, then there might not be too much mutual gain, especially if you are both just starting out, as it will be a case of the blind leading the blind.

- Do they have the same or different business issues? Finding someone with similar issues to you can help a lot. A burden shared becomes a burden halved, and while the underlying issue might be similar, there is a strong probability that each party is struggling with different aspects of it and so can learn from one another. If not, at least two brains are better than one for finding the solution.
- Do they have the same skills? I'm talking about Lean skills here. It makes sense to find a company which has complementary but different skills to you; that way you can leverage each other's knowledge and skills to mutual benefit.
- Are they willing and able to share? The building of a strong relationship depends on openness. If one of the parties is restricted in what they can divulge to the other in terms of ways of working or access to real examples, the relationship will be less beneficial. This means that a potential partner probably would neither be in the same industry nor a competitor; in addition, some companies engaged on government or military work might have restrictions on what they can share. This is not to say that these situations should be avoided, it just means that you need to understand what can and can't be disclosed and if this makes a difference to you. If not, then fine, no problem.

At the end of the day, however, there are no golden rules. Just like in personal relationships, it's about what feels right and taking the relationship slowly at first.

Best practice reference visits

These tend to happen as a forerunner of a partnering relationship, but not always. As a point of reference to establish if the principles are sound, this is a good place to start. In most cases, best practice visits are arranged for you though an institution, forum or consultant rather than setting them up yourself. It's not impossible to do it yourself, but not that easy either. Essentially, this is about going on a visit for a day or two to another company to see and hear how they do things, then bringing that learning back home. It all sounds very logical and simple, but if not planned and managed carefully can be a complete waste of time and effort for all concerned. Why? Because unless you know what you are looking at and then can convert what you see into the context of your own environment, it just ends up as a day out.

Consider this as an everyday parallel. You're on holiday visiting a city, museum or some other cultural attraction in a country you've never visited before. After a day of walking around and looking at the buildings, statues and displays, how much do you really know about the place and the relevance to your home? Not much probably; after the third building, which looks very much like the last two, you start to switch off. Now add in a tour guide who explains what you are looking at, and the interest level and understanding go up quite a lot, but still, the relevance is missing. It's just pot luck if the tour guide happens to talk about the parts in which you have a specific interest. To get the most out of it, you need to do some research first, find out a little about the place, make a note of the parts that interest you and have some questions prepared to get more detail where you want it. Now you come back from holiday full of the place.

It's the same for best practice visits: you need to do your homework! Again, here are a few questions to ask yourself to help get the most out of it:

- Are the activities that are going on or the products relevant to you? This doesn't mean that it needs to be exactly the same, but you need to be able to relate what you're seeing to your own environment. It would probably not make sense to visit an insurance company if you make tractors, an extreme example I know, but you know what I mean.

- What parts of the operation do we want to see and learn about? Most businesses are quite complex and have a lot going on. Without some filtering and focus, the part you want to see might get lost in a sea of stuff that is of little interest to you, or even get missed completely. Figure out what you are interested in and explain this to the people you're visiting.

- Is there enough time to prepare properly? Plan well ahead and liaise constantly with an organiser of the place you're visiting. People are generally quite busy and the very person who is the fount of all knowledge on the subject you want to know about might be unavailable. Setting up a visit for someone is a lot of work: coordinating people to be available, organising a tour of the facility, preparing materials to give out or present take a lot of time and effort and can't be done at the drop of a hat. Also, you and the visit team will need to prepare a series of questions to ask.

- Who should go and who should not? Selecting the people who are to go on the visit from your company needs very careful thinking about. You don't want to send an army; on the other hand, just sending one person is probably a waste of time too. Also, who you send is very important. You need to match the participants to the things that you want them to learn. In a lot of cases there will be a real mix here of technical skills, practical skills and management learning to be had. Let this drive your selection, not pressure from people who think they should or have a right to go. This sounds very obvious, but unless you are using some hired help to organise things, it can be difficult.

- How are we going to capture what we learn? Remember, in most cases, you are only going to get one shot at this. OK, you might be able to follow up with a one-on-one call to clarify a few points after the event, but you won't be getting a revisit to cover the same ground. Therefore, you need to make sure the individual people going are fully aware of what they are going to be responsible for in terms of asking questions and recording what they see and hear. It makes sense to have a bit of redundancy here, two brains thinking about a subject can see and learn a lot more than one with the same input material. Also, someone will need to manage and do the collating of all the notes and create a "Learnings" document for distribution. There will certainly be the need for a visit team debrief once you get back home.

Forums, blogs and social media

The most rapidly growing method of sharing experiences is forums, blogs and social media. While these have been around for a while, the explosive growth of the Internet and social media over recent years has made this much more accessible to a lot more people. Now you can simply type in a question and in seconds have access to a huge number of forums and individual opinions on just about anything from a solution to a specific issue to high-level strategic direction. Given this, it is almost a dead certainty that someone out there has had or is having the same issue as you and started a community forum of similar people or companies to discuss it.

Also, once you've made the connection, you can exploit it further by maintaining a dialogue on the subject or starting up another thread on a different subject. These forums offer a wealth of free insights and very often have links to published papers, webinars and conference events.

While these are extremely valuable sources of information, they should carry a bit of a health warning. Most forums have moderators who filter the content to some extent; however, this does not guarantee that the advice or opinions expressed are correct. You really need to do your homework and get opinion from multiple sources to validate that what you're hearing is sound advice or knowledge. Even with this done, you will need to translate it into the context of your own situation.

Institutions

One way to overcome the risks of getting burned by bad advice through using the above is through recognised institutions like the Lean Institute, the Lean Six Sigma Institute, the Demand Driven Institute and the Lean Enterprise Academy, among others. These all have much more thorough moderation, formal membership and established credibility. While all of this does not provide a guarantee that you'll always get good information, the chances are much higher, leaving only the interpretation to your own environment to do. Within these there are usually a number of discussion groups which converse on specific topic areas, with recognised subject matter experts running discussions and making regular contributions.

Doing a bit of research and joining a couple of these can very often pay huge dividends. Most are free to join, but some do have a "premium" membership which gives you access to contact details, white papers, tools and other useful materials not available to the free membership. In addition, many institutions organise and host conferences and seminars with guest speakers and opportunities to network.

Before I finish up on this section there is one comment I'd like to make. The funny thing about all these types of collaboration is that companies are usually not too concerned about the loss of competitive advantage by sharing, particularly if the sharer is more advanced on the journey than the receiver. Although, even in these cases, the giving is very rarely one way. The reason for this can be summed up by a conversation I had a while ago with one of the leaders from Toyota. Toyota readily shares its learning in many ways, including showing working examples of what they are doing and how it works, even to their direct competitors. I was more than a little surprised by this, so asked if they were concerned about giving away their competitive advantage. The response was very simple: "No, not really. You see, even if we tell them about our latest Lean innovations, by the time they have interpreted them to suit their business and then implemented them, we will have moved on and be even better." It makes you think, doesn't it?

Don't try this at home!

How could I not mention this, given what I do for a living? While it may seem like a bit of a plug for my own chosen profession, I'll try not to be too biased and attempt to provide you with some advice on how to wring the most out of the hired help for the least amount of outlay. I can almost hear the other Partner in our firm screaming in anguish already!

While the title of this section might seem a little trivial, there is a serious point to be made here. When you go on the courses or see someone else's accomplishments or read the books, it all seems so simple you would think anyone could do it. To some extent this is true, but there's no substitute for experience. As is the case for any major change in life or business, it doesn't come easy and there are a lot of bear traps just waiting to be stepped on by the unwary.

Getting advice and help from someone who has been there, done that, got the T-shirt along with the grey hairs and battle scars can save you a lot of pain and false starts in the long run. That "someone" usually takes the form of a consultant (or two!). Now, you could find and employ an experienced person to fulfil this role for you, and indeed, many do. However, the advantage of a consultant is just that, they're used to helping companies through change and usually have more than just technical skills. Also, it's easier to find a consultant firm that can offer the blend of skills and experience you are looking for than it is to find an individual with all these skills to employ. Given all of this, it usually makes economic sense in the long run to use a consulting firm to help you, even taking into account the extortionate fees they might be charging you. However, this is only true if you use the consultant in the right way. Having been on both sides, I have put a few insights below on how to do this and get the best value from the help. One thing to remember at all times is the role of consultants. They are a catalyst, they are there to advise, influence and facilitate change but have no direct control over the process; that is the role of the business leadership and you.

Reasons to hire and not to hire a consultant

Let's first look at whether you should be hiring a consultant in the first place, starting with the wrong reasons.

The don'ts
Reason 1 – A consultant is not there to do your work for you   There are a couple of main reasons people hire consultants to do the work:

> "We don't have the resources, we need some extra hands to get the work done."

> "We need to focus on the business while the project gets done."

All sound very familiar? Probably; I've come across these so frequently it's untrue, not just in Lean. A project gets kicked off by senior leadership, the organisation looks around at the limited resources and other stuff that needs to get done, then gets on the phone to find someone to pull off the project. The outcome of all this is very obvious, but it's amazing how often it happens anyway. Project gets done on time, consultant gets paid, consultant goes away, everything unravels because no one in the business understands anything about what the consultant has done. The consultant then gets the blame, which to be fair, is partly right, as any good consultant should insist on the right level of involvement from their clients.

If the real reason is truly the two statements above and not a capability issue, then you would be better off hiring some extra people to do the work and keeping it in the family rather than using a consultant. Even here, there will be a tendency to isolate the project team while the business-as-usual continues, which should be avoided.

Reason 2 – A consultant is not there to fix your problems Closely linked to the above reasons, a consultant is not a silver bullet on which to offload all your woes and ills so they can fix them. Yes, a consultant can help you identify and solve problems, and indeed this is their role, but it's still your problem, not theirs. You have to understand what the problem is and how it's being fixed, otherwise you won't be able to fix the problem again if it pops up in another guise in the future.

Reason 3 – Add credibility to the boss's decision Again, I've had this happen to me as a consultant, been put in the position of a nodding donkey when the COO says what he wants doing. While this is OK if you actually agree with what he is saying, it shouldn't be the going in position. As a client you should be willing to let the consultant review the facts and circumstances and come to conclusions on the best course of action. If you don't agree, then have a healthy debate on the matter and either come to agreement or agree to disagree. At the end of the day, you are the client; the consultant will give their point of view. It's up to you if you act on it or not.

Now we've covered the "why nots", let's look at a few reasons why you might want to hire a consultant.

The dos

Reason 1 – To inject experience and specific skills into the team It's inevitable that as you start out on your journey you are going to be lacking some of the skills and knowledge you need in terms of strategy and use of tools. A consultant can plug these gaps and stop you reinventing the wheel. If you've gone to the right people for help, they will have been in this position before and will know how to go about it and some of the right tools to use. They will also have templates and worked examples to help. However, be aware that your situation will be unique to some extent, so they won't have all the answers in the bag to just pull out when needed.

Reason 2 – Providing an outside perspective   How many times, in every walk of life, have you wondered if you are doing the right thing? And how reassuring is it when someone who has been there before gives you the benefit of their experience, even if this tells you that you weren't entirely on the right track?

Also, "not seeing the wood for the trees" comes into play here. If you're wrapped up in the everyday trials and tribulations of the business, it is often very difficult to see a different perspective on life. This is where getting an external view can be very helpful to set you off in a different direction.

Reason 3 – To influence and coach leaders in the right direction
No matter how progressive your company claims to be, there will always be a reluctance to be fully open and honest about messages going upwards. Also, a company's culture will be deeply embedded and not necessarily conducive to the new ways of working that a Lean environment requires. This is where a good consultant can really come into their own. Being an outsider, they are not as constrained by the company hierarchy or functional silos as someone from within. Therefore, they can give the messages that are difficult to get across, especially if these messages are about behaviour. It's not just about giving the message either, they can provide coaching and support at all levels while the new ways of working are still in their infancy and vulnerable to the misplaced and inappropriate word.

Reason 4 – Getting out of the failure hamster wheel   Nothing is really new. Lean certainly isn't. At the time of writing this book, Lean could almost be considered "old hat". Therefore, it's almost inevitable that something like this has been tried before and may have failed. Sometimes many times. Once you've been through this cycle a couple of times, it can be very difficult to get any traction at all for having another go, even if you are trying something different. Also, if you've tried and failed before, there will have been a reason for it. The chances are, the reasons for the failure will still be there this time around, so the result will very likely be the same unless something changes. A consultant can add the something extra and different to start out on a new track, or provide the credibility to the solution that convinces the naysayers to give it another go.

Getting the right help

Once you've established that you really do need the help of a consultant, here are a few tips for getting the right help.

Tip one – You are engaging people not firms

Just because the business card has one of the big name consulting firm's logos on the front doesn't automatically mean that the person facing you is the right person for the job.

In most cases, there will be some sort of meeting or presentation to back up the proposal for the work. This is your time to test the credentials of the people in the room, not the firm as a whole. I'm sure the presentation is full of case studies which will be very impressive, but there are two critical questions you must ask:

> "Can each of you explain the role you personally played in these case studies?"

> "Have you worked together on a project before and is it one of these?"

At this point, you may well get a long, pregnant pause and a few worried looks exchanged between the people facing you. If, however, you are satisfied that the people here are indeed good, experienced and right for you, then there is one final and crucial question to ask:

> "Are you people here in this room going to be the people working on the project?"

Now, while a consulting firm can never absolutely guarantee individuals' availability, there should be some commitment that they won't send the school bus to your door full of inexperienced staff overseen by one part-time senior person. This sounds very cynical, I know, but I've seen it happen more than once and it never ends well for the client or the consultant.

While on the subject of this tip, don't just consider the established "big firm" names. There are quite a few boutique consulting firms out there which specialise in this type of work and are very, very good. The advantages of using one of these are many: they will almost certainly have a lot of experience, usually gained at one of the big consulting firms and in industry; the people showing up for the meeting almost certainly will be the people doing the work; the fee rates are generally a bit lower for the same level of expertise. One word of caution on this approach: unless the work is very limited either in time or scope, be careful of the one-man band. While the individual might have all the right credentials, there might be a bandwidth issue if the project starts to grow or he gets diverted by another client while working for you. This is not to say don't go here, but just be aware of what you're taking on.

Tip two – Be very, very clear on what you want the consultant to do

Before starting out, both parties need to be very clear on expectations and what is being done. Failure to do this will end in tears for all and bad feeling. This definition should include: the business areas and geographies to be covered; specific processes or functions to be supported; the nature of the changes expected; consultant roles and project team roles and accountabilities (doing, coaching, facilitating, etc.); and a list of "deliverables" (I hate that word – I'm not even sure it is a word!), which the consultant will be expected to contribute to or prepare. A good consultant will help you on this one as part of the proposal process, as they will have the scars from not doing this in the past. At the end of the day, though, it is your responsibility to define very clearly the boundaries of what you want the consultant to do.

Tip three – Make the consultant accountable for knowledge transfer

This links back to the reasons for hiring a consultant. It has to be recognised that at some point the consultant will walk out of the door and leave you to it. Unless they have transferred the skills and knowledge to your team before they leave, the chances are that all the hard work and anguish expended on getting to where you are will start to unravel. It is imperative that skills and knowledge transfer is made part of the deal from day one, and that the consultant is aware of their accountability to do this. This is probably the only thing that the consultant is accountable for. Some mechanism to test this needs to be in place and progress needs to be monitored as the project or programme proceeds.

Setting this expectation can certainly sort out the good from the mediocre consultant, as the skills to teach, coach and nurture to build capability in an organisation are a lot more than just knowing the tools and processes.

Tip four – Have skin in the game on both sides

This one can be a bit of a stretch, particularly if it is the first encounter between the consultant and you. What I'm talking about here is asking the consultant to put their money where their mouth is. All consultants will assure you that they are completely confident that with their help you will be successful and the benefits will be delivered in spades. So, test this by asking them to put some of their fees at risk based on the results. Many of the big firms will not even consider this as it will not pass muster with their risk assessment process and, if they do, the base fee rate will go through the roof. However, many of the smaller firms may be willing to do this. How much will depend on the specifics of the situation and the risks involved.

However, this is not a one-sided deal, there needs to be something in it for the consultant too. Usually this has a financial element and a control element.

Let's deal with the financial element first. To enter into this potentially risky situation, the deal must allow for the consultant to make more money than the typical time-and-materials contracts. Good delivery must provide a premium for them and exceptional delivery must give a real boost.

The other element of these deals is the control side. Remember what I said above about the role of the consultant? Well, in this case, the consultant must have some control over the decisions made. Usually, there is a clause in the contract that stipulates that the client should act on the advice given and if they don't the contract reverts to a time-and-materials basis. After all, it's not fair to ask the consultant to put their livelihood on the line if you're not going to hold up your side of the deal.

In conclusion

So that just about covers the subject on getting help. There are good reasons to get some help in one form or another, but it's not a requirement. In the end it's your decision on if, what and how you get some help. The above should give you some guidance on what is available and how to use it to the best advantage.

14

RESULTS, WHAT TO EXPECT AND WHAT IS POSSIBLE

B efore I sign off and call it a day on this book, there is one last thing to do. Up to now, we've been talking about concepts and principles, tools, techniques and creating the environment for success. I've also hinted a few times at what the benefits might be, but not really spelled them out. Well, now's the time to set that record straight; after all, it's a lot of effort to go to if there is no return for that investment.

The statements on benefits made here are based on years of personal experience as well as benchmarks and studies made by external third parties. Yes, they're averages and we all know how misleading they can be, but it should give you some idea of what to expect. To get the real low-down on what it's all going to be worth to you, you'll need to do a business case. See Chapter 9 on this subject for more details.

Benefits fall into two major buckets, which we will explore in a bit of detail below, starting with the ones most people have top of their list: "Show me the money!" After that, we'll take a look at some benefits of a more personal nature, which will go a long way to helping sustain the changes and keep your hands on the money long into the future.

It's also worth noting that these benefits are what should be expected after the initial transformation stage, in other words, 18–24 months for a large company, earlier for a smaller one. Let's not forget that Lean is a never-ending journey based on a series of step changes with continuous improvement in between.

Financial benefits

These all end up in the same place in the long run: improving the bank balance and making shareholders happy. As usual we are going to start with the customer.

Revenue enhancement

Selling stuff isn't just about having a good product and good sales people; keeping customers is about making sure that they get what they want when they want it. If you can do this better and more reliably than the next guy, then you are going to keep your customers and steal some of the other guy's when they fail.

A well-designed and implemented Lean supply chain will deliver on time and in full better than an un-Lean one. Why? Because you're focused on what is needed to guarantee service: making to order or replenishing a calculated strategic buffer. You're not wasting time and effort doing something that might not be needed at the expense of something that is needed. Also, Lean supply chains tend to be more resilient to the unexpected, so when something does happen out there and the customer orders double the normal, the whole system reacts in line with it, protecting supply and making sure the orders are filled. On-hand inventory levels might get a bit scary initially, but that's what it's for.

Looking back, you might remember that there was a major part of this book devoted to flow and maintaining flow. Indeed, flow is one of the fundamentals of Lean. What flow does is dramatically reduce lead times, usually by 50% and very often more. This allows you to respond to new customer demand and get new products to market much more quickly, extending the life of a new product and beating the competition to the punch with new customers and markets entering the fray.

All of this can have a very significant impact on the revenue line of the P&L account. Depending on how big your margins are and the ratio of variable to fixed costs, even a modest increase in revenue can have an enormous impact on profits. To underline this, let's take a look at the numbers for a typical consumer packaged goods manufacturer.

Operating margins tend to be quite small, usually in the 25–30% range, with other non-operating costs reducing this to 5–10%. Variable operating costs are also usually quite low as materials are cheap, but the fixed costs of manufacturing and distribution infrastructures and organisations tend to be quite large by comparison.

Let's say that sales are $1 million and overall profits are 10%, or $100k. Let's also say, for the case of argument, variable costs are 40% of total costs and that Lean increases sales by 10%, which is actually quite conservative for a fast-moving industry. The extra $100k of sales only increases total costs by the variable amount (40% of $90k), which equals $36k. The fixed costs stay the same, assuming that you could absorb the additional volume with the current asset capacity. The other $64k of revenue bypasses all the other P&L lines and lands straight on the bottom line profit, making it $164k or a 64% increase in profit. Not bad, eh? It's for this reason that Lean should not be considered a cost-cutting tool, as usually the revenue opportunities massively outweigh the cost reduction benefits.

Cost reduction

This leads us nicely on to cost reduction, which has many facets in the transition from the non-Lean to the Lean world.

The primary basis for cost reduction in Lean is that you stop doing stuff you can't sell. This can take many forms: process steps that get simplified or disappear altogether; fewer handoffs and briefings causing duplication of effort; sharper decision making; fewer mistakes and subsequent reworking; buying or providing products or services that aren't needed by the customer and end up using warehousing space and eventually being thrown or given away. The list just goes on and on until you run out of breath.

But all this does not come about by actively reducing costs. All this is due to understanding value and flow and aligning both to the customer. In other words, much of this comes from our good old friend the value stream map. In addition, it's important to understand that savings have a cumulative knock-on effect. Making a well-thought-through change in one area can manifest savings in a multitude of others without actively doing anything there at all. For example, let's say that you figure out a way to join two parts of a manufacturing process together, which will improve the flow. Before the change, the output from step one needed to be moved away to be stored for a while before being brought back to be worked on again in step two. On its own, the lead time improvement will give you benefits, as described in the section above, which is good and probably the primary reason for the change. But, let's dig a little deeper. If the steps are not joined up, there is no need to pay people to move it back and forth to the storage location, so there's a saving right there. In addition, storing it used to take up space in a warehouse which is no longer needed and can be got rid of. You had to pay for the materials to make it; while it's sitting in the warehouse, the customer won't pay for it, so you have to take money from the bank to pay the supplier and are losing interest on that money. Accidents happen, every once in a while something gets damaged moving it in and back out of storage, meaning that it has to be repaired or made again. You see, all these knock-on savings all arose from one change made to improve flow. The last one is actually quite important as it shows how overall quality can improve with Lean as well.

All of this backs up a mantra made earlier about Lean: Lean is about focusing on customer value and flow. If you take care of these, cost reduction is a by-product not a primary driver. However, this "by-product" typically equates to 15–20% of operating costs. Hmm... not bad for a by-product.

Cash flow

The final financial benefit area is cash flow and free cash. At one time, success was all about profitability. As long as there was a margin, all was good. Times have changed and with funding becoming more and more difficult to get, even if interest rates are low, cash is now the new king. This is where Lean really scores a home run. One of the prime targets for Lean is working capital, the cash tied up in the business funding time from when you pay suppliers and staff for materials and work done, to when the customer pays for the products or services provided. If you ignore any impact on payables and receivables for the moment, working capital equates to inventory, which equates to end-to-end lead time. As we've mentioned before, Lean usually cuts this end-to-end lead time by 50% through a combination of improved flow through the conversion processes and reducing raw material and finished good stocking levels. Now let's take the company above as an example and throw a few more typical numbers around. Before Lean, there was about one month of raw material inventory, conversion lead time was two months end-to-end, which is actually quite good, and the markets were holding one month of finished stock. This makes a total end-to-end lead time of four months. Again, the only real costs associated with this are the variable costs, so the cash tied up here is one third of a year's variable cost which equals $1 million $\times$ 40% $\times$ 1/3 = $133k. Now, if we apply the average Lean benefit of a 50% reduction in end-to-end lead time, this puts $67k in the bank. The speed at which you can deliver this is dependent on the flexibility of your supply chain capacity. If you can turn off suppliers and have a large temporary or contract workforce, this can be done very quickly indeed, otherwise it has to be carefully planned.

Now, we said that we would ignore payables and receivables previously, but there can be an impact here as well. With improved service and flexibility to customers and more reliable, smoother demand on suppliers, there might be an opportunity to negotiate more favourable payment terms at both ends, which will cut the working capital even more. This is exactly what one large electronics company managed to do in the extreme. By shortening the lead time, getting customers to pay on order, and holding suppliers to 60 days from receipt, they managed to get the money for the finished products before they paid the suppliers for the materials and services used to make them; they actually had a negative working capital for a while.

Non-financial benefits

These are commonly termed intangible or soft benefits as it's hard or impossible to put a cash value to them. While the primary targets here are more about people and the planet, hard cash again raises its head. Creating the good place to be encourages more commitment and care, which will have an impact on the money at the end of the day. Again, the list is not exhaustive; I'm sure you can think of a number of others, but here are a few to consider.

Safety

In a mature Lean world, there is a strong sense of ownership and discipline. This culture spills over into everything. Also, Lean brings order in terms of a proper place for everything through 5S; visibility through visual controls; and much less of everything in the workplace through better flow, clear roles, responsibilities and accountabilities. These things alone will significantly reduce the probability of an accident, as there is less stuff in the way. If you add to this people who care about how things are done and are consistent in the way that things are done, you end up with a big impact on safety.

Job satisfaction

This is a big one that happens every time with well-implemented Lean. While initially people can see Lean as a threat, once they get used to the changes, there is no going back for most people; indeed, if attempted you'd probably have a riot on your hands!

So why the change in attitudes? When you think about it, all starts to become more clear. At the risk of annoying you all, I'll repeat again what Lean is: a focus on customer value and flow. The value part of this means that what everyone does has a bearing on the customer no matter what their role, and if you think that what you do is worthwhile to somebody, you feel a whole lot better about doing it, as tedious as it might seem. Flow means getting rid of all the stops, starts and distractions that get in the way. Ask most people what they hate most about doing anything, they'll probably tell you about how they want to get on but can't because so-and-so keeps stopping or breaks down or can't be found. Most people's idea of a good day is a busy but trouble-free time.

Finally there is responsibility. Nobody likes to feel like a slave, having to do what they're told without question or necessarily understanding why. In a Lean organisation, people have a lot more autonomy to make decisions that impact what they do as long as the goals are achieved. To enable this, people have to understand the "Why" as well as the "What". Now people have a lot more control over their own destinies, even if the targets are tougher.

With all these benefits, it's no wonder Lean provides a better place to be. Here is an example of what I mean. A short while ago, I was revisiting a company that had started implementing Lean three years earlier. As part of the visit, I got the opportunity to ask a mixed group of people from one of the process execution teams how things were different. All said that things were simpler, that they felt much more in control now. They also said that they were working harder than they were before and had more responsibilities. This made me a little concerned and I said that I would mention this to the site leadership at the visit sum-up. I almost got lynched there and then. To a person, the message was loud and clear: "Don't you dare tell them that we should go back to the old ways of doing things. If you do and they change it all back, we're resigning, then we're coming after you." It was all good natured really, but I considered myself duly put in my place!

Environment

Elimination of the causes of waste is one of the key tools of Lean. In Chapter 2, we talked a bit about the seven categories of waste: Motion, Waiting, Overproduction, Overprocessing, Defects, Inventory, Transportation. If you manage and eliminate these at source, the bottom five will all positively impact the environment.

Eliminating overproduction saves the materials, energy and other resources used. Complex processes tend to use more energy to accomplish and definitely use more time. Less time working means the facilities like lighting, heating and so forth are all operating for shorter periods. Defects create waste materials and consumables just like overproduction; in addition, defective goods getting to the market might be less efficient in operation. Inventory uses energy to move around and to store, and transportation is pretty obvious in its impact on the environment. I'm sure if you think hard enough, you can come up with a positive environmental impact of reducing the other two wastes as well.

OK, I admit, some of these are a little tenuous but I've seen government grants petitioned for and won on much flimsier evidence! It's because of the explanations given above that I don't agree with the campaign for the eighth waste, as I believe that it is an outcome of managing the others. Maybe not a politically correct view, but there you go.

Avoidance of ... whatever

This kind of sits in the middle between financial and non-financial. To be sure, if you avoid something, there is almost always going to be a cash benefit, but for most things, it's rather difficult to put your finger on exactly how much. Hence, sitting on the fence. So, what are we talking about avoiding here?

The obvious one is capital expenditure on capacity for whatever – new production, warehousing, office space, computer equipment and so on. As a result of Lean's elimination of waste, as mentioned above, the load on capacity drops, sometimes quite significantly for the same usable output. What this means is that investment in new capacity, assuming you are growing that is, can be delayed or avoided completely. Sometimes it's hard to prove this and put a solid number on it unless you had already budgeted for an expense and can now cancel or delay it.

The other main avoidance category is risk avoidance. Many companies, and individuals for that matter, make provision for bad days and risks, or get clobbered occasionally by something going wrong. For example, in today's world, customers are asking for guarantees of quality and delivery to the point that if you fail, they not only will ask for their money back and not buy your products or services again, but they will also be looking for compensation in terms of penalties. This is particularly true in sectors that are dominated by tenders where these penalties can be crippling. With the greater control and predictability delivered by Lean, the risk of falling foul of a penalty is reduced. Other risks that are mitigated to a greater or lesser extent by Lean are in the compliance, health, safety and environment areas.

So what's in it for me?

OK, let's switch gears a bit. That's all very well and good for businesses, but what about you? If you apply some of the ideas touted here in your own life, both inside and outside of the work environment, what's it worth to you?

For one thing, you're going to be a lot better organised and more efficient at what you do. That will give you more time to do what you want to do, rather than what you need to do. Unlike me, you won't be getting all worked up looking for that one tool you need to finish a job only to find it an hour after you've given up and packed everything away.

Being a "Lean head" at home and work does have a few drawbacks though. Not really for you, if you're fairly thick-skinned, but for all the people around you. Living or working with someone who insists on 5S everywhere and standard ways of doing things can be intolerable. So if you are one of these, then please be aware that not all of us are perfect and make some allowances!

In conclusion

So, we've covered an array of potential benefits here, but in summary for those who like just the headlines, this is what is typically seen after the initial transformation stage of a Lean journey:

- Service levels meeting or exceeding targets.
- Overall live inventory levels lower by 30–50%.
- Slow-moving and obsolete inventory almost eliminated.
- Factory lead times reduced by 50–70%.
- Overall end-to-end supply chain lead times reduced by 30–50%.
- Response time to new customer demand and new product launches halved.
- Overall cost of goods sold reduced by 15–20%.
- Simpler and more efficient direct and indirect processes with greater repeatability.
- Clear roles and responsibilities.
- More engaged and energised staff.

The list actually goes on, but I think you get the picture. Yes, Lean does seem to deliver the goods, as long as you take care of the basics and sustainability issues talked about in earlier chapters. In many cases the very things you have spent years trying to get by direct means, like cost savings and safety, you get as by-products from Lean without actively having to go after them.

So, are we done? Well, not quite. The title of this chapter is what to expect and what's possible. So far we've talked about what to expect. What is actually possible is a bit trickier as no one has yet got to the end of their Lean journey. However, the history books on Lean tend to indicate that all the above benefits can be repeated again every five years or so, which seems hard to believe until you remember the result of the value-adding to non-value-adding ratio from your value stream map. When you think of it this way, actually it doesn't seem quite so unbelievable, does it? In reality, very few actually manage to do this repeatedly, as human nature and changing markets and leadership rarely allow such a consistent and almost obsessive focus on anything over a time period measured in decades. Even Toyota, who have been at it for this kind of time, probably have not given it the absolute attention they did at the outset. However, please don't lose sight of the fact that this is possible.

15

IN CONCLUSION

As I've used "In conclusion" as a wrap up to all the chapters in this book, it felt only right to finish the book with the same approach, with a final few words before I draw a line under it.

This was never intended to be the definitive book on Lean, exploring all the ins and outs and providing you with everything you need to take you to the destination on your Lean journey. Only you can ever know what that destination might be, and I'm certainly not able to provide you with everything you need, even if I had the space. No, it is intended as a taster, to whet your appetite for greater things and learning by having a go; there's no substitute for practical experience and learning on the job.

Lean is about simplicity and making things easier. Like a lot of good things, it's mainly common sense rather than deep understanding. There are a handful of tools, easily mastered, that will get you a long way. If you do get a bit stuck there are plenty of ways to get a bit of help or advice – you can even give me a call if you like.

If you've got this far and are reading this, it means that you have been interested enough to keep with it, or you've done the detective novel spoiler thing and gone to the last page to see whodunit. If it's the former, I'm glad you found it interesting and useful; if it's the latter, shame on you!

So, go ahead, start the rest of your journey with this beginning, either in work or your real life, and just amaze yourself with what you can do – you can do it!

Appendix

GLOSSARY

In this appendix, I'm going to attempt to define a few of the common terms used in Lean and Six Sigma, both in the more professional way and, as par for this book, more everyday terms. If you're a well-versed practitioner of the art, please don't get too offended at the latter, it's really just a bit of fun! Not all the terms here are used or referenced in this book, but you might come across them as you move forward. Likewise, this is not an exhaustive list either.

*Many thanks to isixsigma.com for some of the "Professional" Definitions

Term	"Professional" Definition*	"Common" Definition
5 Whys	The 5 Whys typically refer to the practice of asking five times why the failure has occurred in order to get to the root cause/causes of the problem. There can be more than one cause to a problem as well.	Being persistent and not accepting the first answer you get as the truth, the whole truth and nothing but the truth. Be careful this doesn't turn into interrogation!

Term	"Professional" Definition*	"Common" Definition
5S	5S is a system for instilling order and cleanliness in the workplace. The Ss stand for: • Seiri – Put things in order (Remove what is not needed and keep what is needed). • Seiton – Proper arrangement (Place things in such a way that they can be easily reached whenever they are needed). • Seiso – Clean (Keep things clean and polished; no trash or dirt in the workplace). • Seiketsu – Purity (Maintain cleanliness after cleaning – perpetual cleaning). • Shitsuke – Commitment (A typical teaching and attitude toward any undertaking to inspire pride and adherence to standards).	1. Everything in its place and a place for everything (once you've cleared out the junk). 2. A way of starting to gain a sense of discipline, which is essential in Lean.
7 Wastes	The 7 wastes are at the root of all unprofitable activity within your organisation.	A way to get your head around all the potential without blowing your mind.
Accountability (c.f. Responsibility)	Conditional personal or professional liability "after" the fact, determined by action or responsibility. Accountability to action assumes the willingness to be held accountable for adequate expertise and capability.	He or she who has one's head on the block if it all goes belly up.

Term	"Professional" Definition*	"Common" Definition
Affinity Diagram	A tool used to organise and present large amounts of data (ideas, issues, solutions, problems) into logical categories based on user-perceived relationships and conceptual frameworking. Often used in the form of "sticky notes" sent up to the front of the room in brainstorming exercises, then grouped by the facilitator and workers. Final diagram shows relationship between the issue and the category. Then categories are ranked, and duplicate issues are combined to make a simpler overview.	Neat way of grouping similar ideas together to cut down on the noise.
Benchmarking	The concept of discovering what is the best performance being achieved, whether in your company, by a competitor or by an entirely different industry.	Checking out what the other guys are doing.
Best Practice	A way or method of accomplishing a business function or process that is considered to be superior to all other known methods.	Ha! No such thing. There may be better practices, but no best practices.
Buffer	The location between each operation in a production line that contains in-process parts. Typically a conveyor, roller-rack or CML continuously moving line.	Anything that acts as a cushion to absorb variability.
Capability	The capability of a product, process, practising person or organisation is the ability to perform its specified purpose based on tested, qualified or historical performance, to achieve measurable results that satisfy established requirements or specifications.	1. Person – You've proved that you know what you are doing. 2. Thing – Does what it says on the tin.

Term	"Professional" Definition*	"Common" Definition
Capacity	The maximum amount of parts that may be processed in a given time period. Is constrained by the bottleneck of the line – that is, the capacity of a production system depends on what is usually the slowest operation. Capacity = 1 / Cycle Time	The most stuff you can pull (or push) through before something goes bang.
Change Agent	A person who leads a change project or business-wide initiative by defining, researching, planning, building business support and carefully selecting volunteers to be part of a change team. Change Agents must have the conviction to state the facts based on data, even if the consequences are associated with unpleasantness.	The person all the rest look to before committing. Good idea to get them on board!
Continuous Improvement (CI)	Adopting new activities and eliminating those which are found to add little or no value. The goal is to increase effectiveness by reducing inefficiencies, frustrations and waste (rework, time, effort, material, etc.).	Never being satisfied. Figuring out and implementing ways of doing something a bit better. Caution: Make sure the thing you're continuously improving is adding value in the first place!
Control Limits	Control limits define the area three standard deviations on either side of the centre line, or mean, of data plotted on a control chart. Do not confuse control limits with specification limits. Control limits reflect the expected variation in the data. Bilateral specification/tolerances have two limits on both sides of the tolerances, which is not appreciated in the unilateral tolerances.	Boundaries beyond which something has changed, or needs changing. Tell you when you need to act.

Term	"Professional" Definition*	"Common" Definition
Critical Customer Requirement	Something which is relevant and required by the customer. A CCR must be both measurable and controllable.	Their definition sounds good to me.
Critical Success Factor (CSF)	The term for an element that is necessary for an organisation or project to achieve its mission. It is a critical factor or activity required for ensuring the success of a company or an organisation. The term was initially used in the world of data analysis and business analysis.	The few things that you are going to be measured on to determine if you get a bonus or get fired.
Customer	A person who receives the product or service of a process. In a layman's language: A customer is one who buys or rates our process/product (in terms of requirements) and gives the final verdict on the same. This, in turn, acts as hidden feedback, which can be implemented, leading to improvement to all the parameters of the process management.	See Chapter 2. The person who is prepared to pay for or sacrifice something else to get your product or service.
Cycle Time (c.f. Lead Time)	The total time from the beginning to the end of your process, as defined by you and your customer. Cycle time includes process time, during which a unit is acted upon to bring it closer to an output, and delay time, during which a unit of work is spent waiting to take the next action. In a nutshell – cycle time is the total elapsed time to move a unit of work from the beginning to the end of a physical process. (Note, cycle time is not the same as lead time.)	How long it takes to make one of anything. Do not confuse with lead time, they are not the same thing!

Term	"Professional" Definition*	"Common" Definition
DFSS	Design for Six Sigma	Designing something that works properly.
DMAIC (DMAIIC)	Define, Measure, Analyse, Improve, (Implement), Control. Incremental process improvement using Six Sigma methodology. Pronounced (Duh-May-Ick). DMAIC refers to a data-driven quality strategy for improving processes, and is an integral part of a company's Six Sigma Quality Initiative. DMAIC is an acronym for five interconnected phases: Define, Measure, Analyse, Improve, (Implement) and Control.	Structured method for driving improvement.
DPMO	Defects per million opportunities (DPMO) is the average number of defects per unit observed during an average production run divided by the number of opportunities to make a defect on the product under study during that run normalised to one million.	A measure of how easy it is to mess something up. The application of Murphy's Law.
Empowerment	A series of actions designed to give employees greater control over their working lives. To invest with power or give authority to complete. To empower employees. Being allowed to make decisions and take actions on your own, apart from management. A contract that involves the delegation of authority and commitment to an individual to act or authorise actions to be taken, in exchange for the acceptance of responsibility and accountability to fulfil a defined objective. Used to increase an organisation's	Anarchy! No, really. But yes, really, if not understood and implemented properly with clear accountability and responsibility boundaries, empowerment = anarchy with disastrous results.

Term	"Professional" Definition*	"Common" Definition
	responsiveness, effectiveness and efficiency without increasing the budget.	
ERP	Stands for Enterprise Resource Planning. ERP refers to software packages that attempt to consolidate all the information flowing through the company from finance to human resources. ERP allows companies to standardise their data, streamline their analysis process and manage long-term business planning with greater ease.	Overly complex method by which software and consulting companies extract enormous amounts of money from your business with little or no overall impact on your profitability. For consistently recording what you've done – Good. For planning and driving what needs to be done now – Bad. There are much simpler ways to do this.
Fishbone Chart	A tool used to solve quality problems by brainstorming causes and logically organising them by branches. Also called the Cause and Effect diagram and Ishikawa diagram.	Linking causes with effects in a diagram that looks like a fish skeleton.
Gemba	Japanese term that means workplace where day-to-day activities are performed.	Fair enough, can't really simplify this.
Heijunka	A Japanese term that means "leveling". Relationship Among Predictability, Flexibility and Stability Is Heijunka. When implemented correctly, Heijunka provides predictability by levelling demand, flexibility by decreasing changeover time and stability by averaging production volume and type over the long term.	Life's always a compromise. This is a method of understanding and quantifying the compromises.

Term	"Professional" Definition*	"Common" Definition
Hoshin Kanri	A step-by-step strategic planning process that assesses breakthrough strategic objectives against daily management tasks and activities. It provides a visual map at all levels of the organisation, providing clear strategic direction. Hoshin Kanri methodology ensures that everyone in the organisation knows the strategic direction for the company. Creating a working communication system means everyone is working towards a common goal! Another key component of Hoshin is the measurement and analysis that takes place in order to base decisions on fact and not gut feelings. Measuring the system as a whole is critical to organisational effectiveness.	Breaking down the big picture into chunks everyone can understand and buy into. Ensures everyone knows their role in the new world.
Just in Time (JIT)	A planning system for manufacturing processes that optimises availability of material inventories at the manufacturing site to only what, when and how much is necessary. Typically, JIT manufacturing avoids the conventional conveyor systems. JIT is a pull system where the product is pulled along to its finish, rather than the conventional mass production which is a push system.	Getting everything to where it's needed when it's needed and not before. Caution: Can end up being JTL, Just Too Late!
Kaizen	Japanese term that means continuous improvement, taken from the words 'Kai' that means continuous and 'Zen' that means improvement. Some translate 'kai' to mean change and 'Zen' to mean good, or for the better.	A bit more structured than Continuous Improvement. Usually takes the form of an event where people involved in the process get together and define a better way, then implement it.

Term	"Professional" Definition*	"Common" Definition
Kanban	A Japanese term. The actual term means "signal". It is one of the primary tools of a Just in Time (JIT) system. It signals a cycle of replenishment for production and materials. This can be considered a "demand" for product from one step in the manufacturing or delivery process to the next. It maintains an orderly and efficient flow of materials throughout the entire manufacturing process with low inventory and work in process. It is usually a printed card that contains specific information such as part name, description, quantity, etc. In a Kanban manufacturing environment, nothing is manufactured unless there is a "signal" to manufacture. This is in contrast to a push-manufacturing environment where production is continuous.	One form of a buffer to smooth out demand and signal the need to do something. Also limits the amount of stuff in the pipe. The fridge – looking in here tells you when you're getting short as well as limiting how much you buy (unless, like me, you have a spill-over fridge in the garage for the beer!)
Kano Analysis	A quality measurement tool used to prioritise customer requirements based on their impact on customer satisfaction. All identified requirements may not be of equal importance to all customers. Kano analysis can help you rank requirements for different customers to determine which have the highest priority. The results can be used to prioritise your effort in satisfying different customers.	A way of finding out how to qualify for the game, stay in the game and beat the competition. Seems to me that the example used in the following "dissatisfiers" has been used as a "must-be" if my flying experience is anything to go by.

Term	"Professional" Definition*	"Common" Definition
	Briefly, Kano (a Japanese researcher) stated that there are four types of customer needs, or reactions to product characteristics/attributes: 1. The "surprise and delight" factors. These really make your product stand out from the others. Example, a passenger jet that could take off vertically. 2. The "more is better: e.g. a jet airliner that uses a little less fuel than the competition. 3. The "must be" things. Without this, you'll never sell the product. E.g. A jet airliner that cannot meet airport noise regulations. 4. Finally, there are the "dissatisfiers", the things that cause your customers not to like your product. E.g. a jet airliner that is uncomfortable to ride in.	
KISS	Keep It Simple and Specific. The term is used for executive summary to management for their information and also for project leaders who might get lost in the complexities of the Six Sigma horizon. The term in itself suggests to apply common sense before selecting any complex tool and landing away from the real world.	Aka Keep It Simple Stupid! A phrase often directed at the team presenting their latest whiz-bang solution to all the world's problems.
KPI	Key Performance Indicator – indicates any key performance that gives the actual data for that particular outcome.	The few things that really make the difference. Not the 20-page list of everything that might have some impact.

Term	"Professional" Definition*	"Common" Definition
Lead Time (c.f. Cycle Time)	The amount of time, defined by the supplier, that is required to meet a customer request or demand. (Note, lead time is not the same as cycle time).	Not to be confused with cycle time. This is the demonstrated time it takes to respond. Including all the interference from having a million other things going on at the same time.
Leader	The person who leads or commands a group, organisation or country.	Someone who gets results from a team or person by inspiring, motivating and giving direction and support. (Not all managers are leaders; not all leaders are in senior positions!)
Lean Manufacturing	Initiative focused on eliminating all waste in manufacturing processes. The Production System Design Laboratory (PSD), Massachusetts Institute of Technology, states that, "Lean production is aimed at the elimination of waste in every area of production including customer relations, product design, supplier networks and factory management. Its goal is to incorporate less human effort, less inventory, less time to develop products, and less space to become highly responsive to customer demand while producing top quality products in the most efficient and economical manner possible."	The MIT part looks OK. Be careful that you're not just squeezing a balloon. Lean Manufacturing can get hung up on what's going on within the walls of a factory to the detriment of the customer and the business as a whole.

Term	"Professional" Definition*	"Common" Definition
Little's Law	Any Lean journey strives to minimise waste and increase speed. Increasing speed equates to reducing lead time to your customers. Minimising waste includes an analysis of inventory on-hand and steps to reduce that inventory. Little's Law provides an equation for relating Lead Time, Work-in-Process (WIP) and Average Completion Rate (ACR) for any process. Named after the mathematician who proved the theory, Little's Law states: Lead Time = WIP (units) / ACR (units per time period) Knowing any two variables in the equation allows the calculation of the third.	Simple: LT = WIP/Output Rate Figure out how to improve one and the others get better.
Measures (c.f. Metrics)	Things to measure to understand quality levels. Metric means measurement. Hence the word metric is often used in an organisation to understand the metrics of the matrix (the trade-off).	Things you measure.
Metrics (c.f. Measures)	Things to measure to understand quality levels. Metric means measurement. Hence the word metric is often used in an organisation to understand the metrics of the matrix (the trade-off).	The opposite is not repeated as a mistake. Very often, measures and metrics are used synonymously. However, metrics have measures, targets and consequences of not meeting them.

Term	"Professional" Definition*	"Common" Definition
MRP	One of the first software-based integrated information systems designed to improve productivity for businesses. A materials requirement planning (MRP) information system is a sales forecast-based system used to schedule raw material deliveries and quantities, given assumptions of machine and labour units required to fulfil a sales forecast.	A very good tool for understanding what you might need in the future at each point in the supply chain so you can get ready for it. A very bad tool for telling you exactly what to make when.
Muda	Japanese word for waste	See Waste below
Noise	A process input that consistently causes variation in the output measurement that is random and expected and, therefore, not controlled is called noise. Noise is also referred to as white noise, random variation, common cause variation, a non-controllable variable.	Background chaos which stops you seeing what's really going on.
OEE	OEE means overall equipment effectiveness. It is a method to find out the overall effectiveness of equipment. It is obtained by multiplication of three ratios. 1. Availability ratio – Time for which equipment was available for operation divided by total calendar period for which OEE is being calculated. 2. Quality ratio – Quantity of "A" grade/Prime grade material produced divided by total production (Off grade+Prime grade) 3. Performance ratio – Rate of production divided by capacity of machine to produce. Normally OEE is presented in terms of a percentage.	A measure of how well you are using a piece of equipment. OEE can be the death of Lean if taken in isolation. BE WARNED!

Term	"Professional" Definition*	"Common" Definition
Opportunity Cost	The cost of an alternative that must be foregone in order to pursue a certain action. Put another way, the benefits you could have received by taking an alternative action.	Difference in cost or lost benefit of not doing something.
Poka Yoke	Japanese term which means mistake proofing. A poka-yoke device is one that prevents incorrect parts from being made or assembled, or easily identifies a flaw or error. Or "mistake-proofing" – a means of providing a visual or other signal to indicate a characteristic state. Often referred to as "error-proofing," poka-yoke is actually the first step in truly error-proofing a system. Error-proofing is a manufacturing technique of preventing errors by designing the manufacturing process, equipment and tools so that an operation literally cannot be performed incorrectly.	Designing something that makes it impossible to get wrong. Example, the nozzle size which stops you putting diesel in a petrol (gas) car. Unfortunately, that example doesn't work the other way round!
Process Owner	The individual(s) responsible for process design and performance. The process owner is accountable for sustaining the gain and identifying future improvement opportunities on the process.	Caretaker for the process. Not necessarily the manager or person doing it, but the one who will ensure it's done right and gets better.
Process Thinking	Surprisingly, this is not very well defined anywhere, so look opposite.	Seeing the bigger picture and understanding what all the levers do when pulled in different ways.
Quality	Quality is a function of loss. The better the quality, the less the loss it causes to society – Taguchi	Up to the required standard. Not necessarily perfect.

Term	"Professional" Definition*	"Common" Definition
Quality Assurance (c.f. Quality Control)	A planned and systematic pattern of all actions necessary to provide adequate confidence that the product optimally fulfils customers' expectations. A planned and systematic set of activities to ensure that requirements are clearly established and the defined process complies with these requirements. "Work done to ensure that quality is built into work products, rather than defects." This is by (a) identifying what "quality" means in context; (b) specifying methods by which its presence can be ensured; and (c) specifying ways in which it can be measured to ensure conformance (see Quality Control, also Quality).	Making sure you produce as few bad ones as possible and figuring out how to check for them.
Quality Control (c.f. Quality Assurance)	Also called statistical quality control. The managerial process during which actual process performance is evaluated and actions are taken on unusual performance. It is a process to ensure whether a product meets predefined standards and requisite action taken if the standards are not met.	Testing against a standard and rooting out the bad ones.
Reliability	The reliability of an item is the probability that it will adequately perform its specified purpose for a specified period of time under specified environmental conditions.	The absence of variability.
Responsibility (c.f. Accountability)	Defined or assumed conditional liability "before" the fact, limited to overt practices. Capacity to be responsible assumes the use of adequate expertise and capability.	The person asked to do the job. Don't confuse with Accountability (head on block remember!)

Term	"Professional" Definition*	"Common" Definition
Segmentation	A process used to divide a large group into smaller, logical categories for analysis. Some commonly segmented entities are customers, data sets and markets. For example, you may collect the cause of defects of a process and place the data into a Pareto chart. The Pareto chart then displays the segmentation... type A defects are 50%, type B defects are 30% and type C defects are 10%. These are possible ways to segment the data.	One size doesn't fit all. Making sure you understand which horses are for which courses.
SIPOC	Stands for suppliers, inputs, process, output and customers. You obtain inputs from suppliers, add value through your process, and provide an output that meets or exceeds your customers' requirements. Supplier-Input-Process-Output-Customer: a method that helps you not to forget something when mapping processes.	A memory jogger and way of documenting to make sure you look at all the parts of a process.
Six Sigma	Six Sigma can be understood/ perceived at three levels: Metric: 3.4 Defects Per Million Opportunities. DPMO allows you to take the complexity of the product/process into account. Rule of thumb is to consider at least three opportunities for a physical part/component – one for form, one for fit and one for function, in the absence of better considerations. Also you want to be Six Sigma in the critical to quality characteristics and not the whole unit/characteristics.	Either: About as likely to happen as winning the lottery. Or: A method of doing things better based on removing variation.

Term	"Professional" Definition*	"Common" Definition
	Methodology: DMAIC/DFSS structured problem-solving roadmap and tools.	
	Philosophy: Reduce variation in your business and take customer-focused, data-driven decisions.	
	Six Sigma is a methodology that provides businesses with the tools to improve the capability of their business processes. This increase in performance and decrease in process variation leads to defect reduction and vast improvement in profits, employee morale and quality of product.	
SME	The Subject Matter Expert is that individual who exhibits the highest level of expertise in performing a specialised job, task or skill within the organisation.	Someone who actually knows what they're doing and might be worth talking to.
	An SME might be a software engineer, a helpdesk support operative, an accounts manager, a scientific researcher: in short, anybody with in-depth knowledge of the subject you are attempting to document. You need to talk to SMEs in the research phase of a documentation project (to get your facts straight) and you need to involve them in the technical validation of your drafts (to make sure that your interpretation of information matches theirs).	

Term	"Professional" Definition*	"Common" Definition
SMED	Single Minute Exchange of Die. One of the Lean tools that reduces the changeover time. It has a set of procedures to be followed for a successful implementation. Some advantages: Setup reduction and fast, predictable setups enable Lean Manufacturing. Setup reduction reduces setup cost, allows small lot production, smooths flow and improves kanban.	The "one right way" and fastest way to change from one thing to the next.
Stakeholder	People who will be affected by the project or can influence it but who are not directly involved with doing the project work. Examples are managers affected by the project, process owners, people who work with the process under study, internal departments that support the process, customers, suppliers and the financial department. Alternative definition: People who are (or might be) affected by any action taken by an organisation. Examples are: customers, owners, employees, associates, partners, contractors, suppliers, related people or located nearby. Alternative definition: Any group or individual who can affect or who is affected by the achievement of a firm's objectives.	Pretty much everybody. Anyone even remotely connected to what you're doing. However, while you should treat all stakeholders equally, remember that some stakeholders are more "equal" than others!

Term	"Professional" Definition*	"Common" Definition
Standard Work	Detailed definition of the most efficient method to produce a product (or perform a service) at a balanced flow to achieve a desired output rate. It breaks down the work into elements, which are sequenced, organised and repeatedly followed. Each step in the process should be defined and must be performed repeatedly in the same manner. Any variations in the process will most likely increase cycle time and cause quality issues. It typically describes how a process should consistently be executed and documents current "best practices". It provides a baseline from which a better approach can be developed, allowing continuous improvement methods to leverage learning. Three necessary components in Standard Work are (1) takt time, (2) cycle time and (3) SWIP (Standard Work-in-Progress).	The "one right way", or at least the "one way" written down and timed so people can repeat it.
Takt, Takt Time	*Takt* is the German word for the baton that an orchestra conductor uses to regulate the tempo of the music. *Takt time* may be thought of as a measurable "beat time", "rate time" or "heartbeat". In Lean, takt time is the rate at which a finished product needs to be completed in order to meet customer demand. If a company has a takt time of five minutes, that means every five minutes a complete product, assembly or machine is produced off the line because, on average, a customer is buying a finished product every five minutes. The sell rate – every two hours, two days or two weeks – is the takt time.	A drum beat. The rate at which you need to make or deliver to keep up with demand. Too slow, unhappy customers. Too fast, unhappy bank manager.

Term	"Professional" Definition*	"Common" Definition
TPM	Japanese management philosophy. Stands for Total Productive Maintenance. Used to increase time between failure (MTBF) or life of machinery.	A systemic approach to monitoring and managing equipment to ensure it only stops when you plan it to.
TQM	Total Quality Management	Not leaving quality to good luck. As above for TPM but focused on reliability and ensuring quality.
Variance	The sum of the squared deviations of n measurements from their mean divided by $(n-1)$. The deviation from what was expected. Deviation from process mean, i.e., away from the target, which often results in extra cost to revert back on target/mean.	A statistical term used a lot to define what you need to do to cater for bad variability (see below).
Variation or Variability	Variation is the fluctuation in process output. It is quantified by standard deviation, a measure of the average spread of the data around the mean. Variation is sometimes called noise. Variance is the squared standard deviation.	There's good variation, for example diversity in a gene pool. Then there's bad variation, temperature of your oven over time. Then again, there's variation that doesn't really matter, like eye colour. In most processes, variation isn't good as it makes the outcome less predictable and quality suffers – usually, not always!
Voice of the … Customer, Business, Process, Employee	The "voice of the customer" is a process used to capture the requirements/feedback from the customer (internal or external) to provide the customers with the best in class service/product quality. This process is all about being proactive and constantly innovative to capture the changing requirements of the	A way of getting the truth about what's needed – GO ASK! But make sure whoever you ask really means what they say.

Term	"Professional" Definition*	"Common" Definition
	customers with time. The "voice of the customer" is the term used to describe the stated and unstated needs or requirements of the customer. The voice of the customer can be captured in a variety of ways: direct discussion or interviews, surveys, focus groups, customer specifications, observation, warranty data, field reports, complaint logs, etc. These data are used to identify the quality attributes needed for a supplied component or material to incorporate in the process or product.	
VSM	Value stream mapping is a paper and pencil tool that helps you to see and understand the flow of material and information as a product or service makes its way through the value stream. Value stream mapping is typically used in Lean, it differs from the process mapping of Six Sigma in four ways: 1. It gathers and displays a far broader range of information than a typical process map. 2. It tends to be at a higher level (5–10 boxes) than many process maps. 3. It tends to be used at a broader level, i.e. from receiving of raw material to delivery of finished goods. 4. It tends to be used to identify where to focus future projects, subprojects and/or Kaizen Events. A value stream map (aka end-to-end system map) takes into account not only the activity of the product, but the management and information systems that support the basic process. This is especially helpful when working to reduce cycle time, because you gain insight into the decision-making flow in addition to the process flow. It is actually a Lean tool.	Good, simple way to visualise and explain what's going on. It has four main components: 1. Process steps and inventory points 2. Data about the process steps and inventory points 3. Information flow used to manage the process 4. A timeline. Don't be fooled by imitations. If it doesn't have all four, it's not a value stream map!

Term	"Professional" Definition*	"Common" Definition
Waste	A process in any activity that does not result in moving the process closer to the final output or adding value to the final output.	Anything that does not contribute to the desired result.
Work in Progress/Process	The amount of work that has entered the process but has not been completed.	Stuff that's started but not finished. A good indicator of flow (or lack of it!).
Z-Factor	Defined in terms of four parameters: the means (μ) and standard deviations (σ) of both the positive (p) and negative (n) controls (μ_p, σ_p, and μ_n, σ_n). Given these values, the Z-factor is defined as: $$Z\text{-factor} = 1 - \frac{3(\sigma_p + \sigma_n)}{|\mu_p - \mu_n|}$$	A statistical multiplier to determine how much of something you need to cover for a certain proportion of outcomes. It's used mainly for inventory calculations to cover a required service level. Don't sweat it, look the value up in a table.

AFTERWORD

Hopefully you have reached this part of the book just before the flight attendant asks you to stow all items, return your seats and tray tables to the upright position and prepare for landing. If not, then I've failed in my mission to write the Lean book of Lean, but as you've made it this far, it can't be that bad!

I hope you found this useful in getting you a little prepared to launch into your change programme. After all is said and done, Lean is simple, or should be. If your solutions are complex or difficult for people to understand and to execute, they are probably wrong and definitely not Lean, so go back and have another think.

This book was not meant to be the definitive book on Lean or turn the reader from an absolute novice into a master practitioner in an afternoon; it takes practice and a few more pages to do that. But hopefully, it has helped you understand what Lean is all about, that it's not rocket science, and the few practical tools and tips provided will help you get started.

A word of encouragement or a kick in the backside to get you going: every minute you spend thinking about doing something but not doing it is one less minute you will benefit from the returns, remember the reference to how precious time is in the "Waste" section of Chapter 2? So, get started as soon as you get off this flight, right now! Whatever you do, it does not have to be perfect, that's why you have continuous improvement. To quote an old colleague of mine, "roughly right, not completely wrong is fine". However long you take analysing and planning, you won't think of every-thing, the best place to learn is in situ.

I'll leave you with one final anecdote from my past. I was fortu-nate enough about 18 years ago to meet one of the prime movers in Toyota's Lean journey, who had been at this stuff for 25 years or more. I asked him: "So, how far on your journey are you after 25 years at it?" He answered: "About half way." By chance I bumped into him again only last year at a conference. Over dinner I reminded him of my previous question and his answer to me, then asked him the same question 17 years on. He answered: "Oh, about half way."

So good luck and thanks for your attention.

INDEX